How I Became The Greatest Dad On Planet Earth

How I Became The Greatest Dad On Planet Earth

A Guide To Single Fatherhood

Dr. Proton

DEDICATION

This book is dedicated to my first-born son, Jasher Harold Baldwin. While each of my children is special to me, Jasher was the defining factor through it all. He was born on June 15, 2017, and was diagnosed with autism shortly after. Even from birth I could tell he was different. His mannerisms and his non-verbal gestures set him apart from his siblings. Even as the oldest child he retains unique characteristics unlike any of his peers. While it has been an extra challenge raising him, I've come to appreciate who he was created to be. He loves unconditional and he is quick to ask for forgiveness when he knows he messes up. He has been the central thread throughout this narrative and without him I doubt this book would ever have been written.

Jasher, my soul was tied to you the day you were born, and I love you with all my heart. Love,

Dad.

Contents

KINDERGARTEN

"I love you, Dad!"

"I love you too, son! With all my heart!"

Today was Jasher's first day of school. He was enrolled in kindergarten at six years old. Jasher was really excited about going to school. The chance to learn new things, make new friends, experience a new adventure. Hard to imagine just three months ago he was still in diapers. Yes, you heard that right, three months ago. I'll get into that later. He had grown in leaps and bounds. I was extremely proud of him. He was my soul tie. I was his everything. And now he was finally going to school.

We were sitting in a line of cars waiting ten more minutes until the school opened up at 7 am. He was sitting in my lap in the driver seat of the car with me, playing tickle games and joking around. I kissed him a bunch of times and bear hugged him until it was time for him to get out of the car.

The teachers walked out and I recorded the entire interaction to have it remembered forever. I gave him one last hug and one last kiss. He wanted to give me a kiss as well. One last embrace. I opened the driver door and he got out with a quick hop and my door shut. He turned to face my open window one last time to stand in place, wave his hand, and say, "Good bye, my dad!"

"Good bye, son! I love you! You have a good day!"

And he was off, guided by a teacher's hand to his classroom. I watched him walk up to the doors as I started to drive off. Looking at my side and rear view mirrors as he walked into the building I sighed a burden of relief. Tears of joy welled up in my eyes as I drove off to work. These past five months had changed my life completely and I looked at my son's education as a token of my sacrifice. The road wasn't over, but half the battle had been won.

I was in the middle of a divorce battle with my now ex-wife. I currently had partial custody with the state where the state of Kentucky would visit my house every day to do a wellness check. Jasher was one of three children that were currently living with me and all their needs were being met my yours truly alone. Their mother had her rights removed from seeing the children except for direct supervision. She was currently looked at as not fit to watch the children. I'll get to that in a bit.

Now it was up to me to not only make ends meet, but to become the hero in my own story so my three young children could survive and thrive. Right now I was just barely scraping by and I was in the trenches. I had gone through many hard times in my life, but this was by far the hardest I've ever gone through. Looking back I don't think I'll ever go through such a challenge as I did during this time, but I made it in the end. This is my story.

Sacrifice everything for the ones you love.

Life is hard. If it were easy, everyone would do it. By the time this book gets published I'll be forty years old. Practically half my life is done if I live to be eighty... which I plan on if I never get hit by a truck. In the past forty years my thirty-seventh year was my most emotionally challenging and my thirty-eighth my most financially challenging. It will stand as a reminder that things could always be worse so always count your blessings.

In my thirty-seventh year I found out my wife was cheating on me. It was a hard blow to my reality, but I forgave her. She cheated on me again and I threatened divorce. I forgave her again. She cheated on me a third time and I forgave her yet again, but told her she was breaking my heart. She cheated on me a fourth time and I threatened divorce again, but forgave her a fourth time. When I turned thirty-eight, the following year, I found out she cheated on me for the fifth and final time, but I felt stuck. I needed help and had no idea who to turn to.

Marriage wasn't always perfect and I didn't always love my wife, but by the second year of marriage I put my everything into the marriage and was determined to make it work. During the entirety of the marriage I never cheated one time. I never even flirted with another woman. I was so devoted to our vows that, even when a woman tried to approach me in my dreams, I would tell her I was married. I was so loyal that I didn't even break my vows in my dreams! Marriage was that important to me.

Marriage only works when both parties are in it for the long haul. It breaks down when one party no longer tries or refuses to make it work between both spouses. When one party sacrifices everything for the marriage and the other party doesn't reciprocate that same sacrifice back, the marriage will fall apart. A house divided against itself cannot stand.

Katie cheated on me one too many times. If a spouse cheats one time, that's forgivable. Some would argue against it, but I still believe it's forgivable. Twice? Three times? At what point does cheating become an abusive relationship? At what point does it become an issue of enabling an alcoholic with drinking? Often times, in church, if a man cheats on his wife he's a dog and needs to fix himself. But if a woman cheats, the husband didn't love the wife enough and he needs to fix himself. By default the men are the ones who are at fault and needs the fixing, not the women.

At what point do we stop believing this delusion? Through my tribulation I've come to realize that some people will always be chronic cheaters and you need to let them go and let God deal with them. A chronic cheater will continue to cheat on you regardless of how much you sacrifice in the relationship. They would have cheated on you regardless of what you did so you need to stop blaming yourself. The first part to recovery is to forgive yourself. You had no fault in your spouse cheating on you. They cheated on you because they had no respect for you. They never loved you. If they loved you, they wouldn't have cheated on you.

How long does it take to recover from infidelity? I believe 18 - 24 months depending on whatever circumstance you're in. While I have my moments of grief, from time to time, I do experience peace for the most part now. While it was hard at first, things have become easier. By the time this book gets published it would have been a full two years since I started the divorce proceedings. I felt it imperative to get my story out there while it was still fresh on my mind. To help as many men possible who are going through what I went through in the pursuit of happiness.

Who Is This Book For?

When I first started writing this I was targeting men from my demographic. Men who are either currently going through a toxic divorce with their soon to be ex-wife, men who have already gone through a divorce, or those men who have not yet experienced divorce, but there's a chance of one in your near future. While this may be my target demographic, I've come to realize this book is more all-inclusive.

Let's face it, single mothers make up the largest demographic of those who have full custody of their children. In America the family courts are heavily one sided to benefit mothers. Family court aside, some families have men who have abandoned their role as father and have left the leading role to the single mom. Single mother households are growing every day and a lot of them are in disarray as to how to properly raise children.

Through much trial and effort, literal blood, sweat, and tears, I have developed much wisdom on how to properly raise a family. While I am just one man, my children are well behaved and well mannered. They are wonderful children in public and very lovable behind closed doors. I have proven myself a great father and leader in my own household. If you are a single mom, this book is still for you.

Throughout this book I will elaborate on my trials, tribulations, and the sacrifices I've had to make along the way. My life resembles that of a Cinderella story. Had it gone any other way I might have lost full custody of my kids, but through much prayer and perseverance I came out on top, ahead, and my children are flourishing.

I will teach you how to be the best parent you can be. It still amazes me, to this day, how many compliments I get about my children. They're all well-mannered, well-loved, and happy children. Among their peers they clean up after themselves and treat others with respect. Every time I pick them up they run to me with open arms yelling, "Daddy!" Every. Single. One of them. Every. Single. Time.

My children love me with everything in their being and I love them. I'm a single father raising three young children on my own and they're flourishing and everyone in my community sees it and is amazed and often times say, "I don't know how you do it, John!" To which I reply, "Routines!" or "Plenty of Discipline, lots of love!"

I've read through different books about parenting and how to better raise your children. Often times these books are written by child psychologists or someone learned in some form of psychology. The psychologist asks the question why and takes test examples from other parents to come to a conclusion. I'm not a psychologist. I'm not going to try to be one. What I am is a man with experience and have figured out what works through my own fight and observation. I have no other title other than "Dad."

I will teach you how to be a great parent. One who your children will admire for years to come. One who they will respect. A parent of envy to your peers when most of your peers look more like buddies to their children. Your children are not your friends, they're your replacement. It is your duty to raise these individuals into well-established role models for future generations. I will teach you how to properly lead them in your household so you won't be disappointed in them when they become working adults.

Lastly, I will teach you how to properly love your children. There is a fine line in discipline and affection you need to figure out on your own.

Every child is different and unique. Not every child will need the same amount of discipline. However every child has specific rules you must enforce in order for them to become model citizens. I will teach you that as well.

It's been a difficult path to lead, but the reward has been so worth it. I love my children. And my children love me. Nothing comes close to genuine love and appreciation. I am loved. My tribe is flourishing. Life is good.

SECTION I

HARD TIMES CREATE STRONG MEN

Out of The Frying Pan, Into The Fire

"Hard times create strong men, strong men create good times, good times create weak men, and weak men create hard times." - G. Michael Hopf

"My dog stepped on a bee."

I laughed. I still remember the Johnny Depp vs Amanda Heard case. Still remember hearing Johnny Depp explain how Heard defecated on his bed sheets and how she threw a bottle at him causing his hand to bleed. Now she was defending herself in court talking about her dog stepping on a bee. What their trial did for men everywhere was open the flood gates to the fact women can be the abusers in the relationship.

Close to my divorce day I started to explain to my buddies at work I was married to Amber Heard 2.0. I even changed her name in my contacts on my phone. I laughed to myself. It was the fastest way for me to explain how my wife was not in her right mind. It was a very toxic relationship and I was in the middle of my own trials and tribulations.

I had been married to Katie for six plus years now. We had three children together and I caught my wife cheating on me for the fifth time. Remind you this was the fifth time I CAUGHT her cheating on me. For all I know, it could have been ten. It could have been a hundred. I could only go off her own confession and my personal detective work. I knew she cheated on me at minimum five times.

I felt trapped. The fear of the unknown was the primary reason I wasn't yet ready to file for divorce. The fact we had three children together was the second reason. The idea of the kids not growing up with both parents scared me. But I was in an abusive relationship. I was already emotionally scarred from the year prior. Had she only cheated one time, I could heal. Every time she cheated on me it was as if she dug the knife back into my heart and turned it. Truth is I couldn't fully heal if I stayed in the relationship.

I never cheated one time in my entire marriage. I was happy I could say that. I was proud of the fact that, through the entire marriage, I took my vows extremely seriously. Till death do us part. Unfortunately a marriage can't hold together when only one party is willing to live by their vows they swore to the other party. My wife had not only betrayed my trust, she spit on my face. She didn't have respect for me nor did she care.

Over the course of the last three years my wife became a master manipulator. She convinced her friends that I was a bad husband and even convinced me that she would change for the better. The only thing she could not lie about was how great of a father I was. I was the sole bread winner of the family and one of the best father figures she ever worked with. I adored my children and they adored me. I truly loved them with all my heart.

I Set A Trap - February 2023

Judges 6:36-40 KJV — And Gideon said unto God, If thou wilt save Israel by mine hand, as thou hast said, Behold, I will put a fleece of wool in the floor; and if the dew be on the fleece only, and it be dry upon all the earth beside, then shall I know that thou wilt save Israel by mine hand, as thou hast said. And it was so: for he rose up early on the morrow, and thrust the fleece together, and wringed the dew out of the fleece, a bowl full of water. And Gideon said unto God, Let not thine anger be hot against me, and I will speak but this once: let me prove, I pray thee, but this once with the fleece; let it now be dry only upon the fleece, and upon all the ground let there be dew. And God did so that night: for it was dry upon the fleece only, and there was dew on all the ground.

It was early in the morning when this passage of Scripture came to my head. I was working alone and I had gone out to the connex, at my job site, to pick up some material. I just couldn't stop thinking about how I was in a Will & Jada Pinkett Smith marriage and I needed to get out. I also thought if there was any chance of saving my marriage. Regardless of what transpired, I still wanted to make the marriage work.

I decided to create a litmus test to see if my wife would fall for the trap. It was a simple test. If she was willing to lie on something so insignificantlysmall, she would be willing to lie on the larger things. If she was going to lie to me with a very insignificant question, who knows what else she would lie about in the future?

I sent her a text: "On your new Facebook profile, do you have your relationship status set to nothing?"

The night prior I had found out she created another secret Facebook account without my knowledge and found she was talking to another man. She had done it several times in the past to cheat and now she was up to her old, bad habits once again.

She sent me back the following: "Yep."

The problem with her response was that she had no idea I already looked at her relationship status. On it she put "single." Not only that, but I saw her message to another friend. One of her friends asked her directly about it: "You put single in your status?"

"Well it's what he wants cause he's acting like we're divorced already." She responded in the text.

The relationship status was only deleted after the fact. By her own admission she blatantly lied to my face by text message. I immediately got angry. "This woman is willing to lie on something so insignificant as a relationship status. What else is she lying about?"

At that moment my litmus test proved true. The fleece was wet. My wife was a liar, a manipulator, and a habitual cheater. I came to my senses and I knew it was time to leave. That was the straw that broke the camel's back. I would no longer try to save the marriage. I would end it and take my children with me. From now on she was not my equal. She was my enemy.

Judgment Day - March 2023

The Bible is very clear that there's a judgment day waiting for us after death. Every man and woman will have to stand trial for the deeds they done while on Earth. When your time is up it's time to face the music. Do not pass go. Do not collect $200.

I remember walking into the lawyer's office, still afraid of the unknown. But I knew I couldn't take anymore of the abuse my wife was putting me through. I had been left a shell of the former man I once was. I was no longer happy. I was always on edge. I felt the need to constantly track my wife's movements on her phone gps location. This wasn't healthy. I wanted to trust my wife fully with wherever she wanted to go, but that trust had been broken too many times to count. It was time for me to stop living in delusion and start getting a grip on reality.

I had withdrawn $2000 from our combined checking account. We hardly had anything saved up. That was from the income tax returns. I figured it would probably cost me $1000 up front and I could use the other $1000 as my starter emergency fund when I opened up a new bank account in my name only. I knew the courts were already against men. If I didn't hire a lawyer, I would be a fool.

Keith was a seasoned lawyer. His desk was big. He wore a pinstriped suits and some expensive dress shoes. I could tell he took his job serious. In the months to come I would also learn he would defend anyone as long as you had the paper. I considered him a sly fox. Witty and intelligent, but taking no sides. He was in it for the money, but once you had him on your side you would almost always win. I needed him on my team.

"Two thousand dollars!" I blerted out as my world became numb. I couldn't hear much of what he was saying after that. It's as if everything went silent and the ringing in my ears picked up. All I had was the two thousand dollars I had withdrawn either. I was only expecting it to cost me one thousand up front. I had no idea it would cost me everything I had. Those few words alone would bare meaning to what I would eventually go through in the coming months.

I heard a small voice, almost audible, speak to me clear as day when the world went silent. "How much is your sanity worth to you?" It was as if God Himself were speaking to me direct. The question stuck in my head. How much was my sanity worth? Everything.

"I'll do it!" Keith stopped talking. "I have $1000 on me cash and $1000 more in my car. I'll do it." He immediately started writing up the paperwork. I laid the money on his desk. Ten minutes later I laid the other thousand on the table. There was only roughly $3000 left in the checking from the income tax returns. I figured I'd withdraw $1500 more and start my new bank account while leaving $1500 for her. 50/50 split.

I got back into my car with the papers to fill out about my information, my address, assets, liabilities, and children. I knew speed was everything. The one who's the fastest to divorce their spouse first is generally treated as the victim in the family court system. If we were going to be divorced I would make sure I was the one to initiate it. I knew my kid's lives were at steak. I was a great father. She was a terrible mother. And within the next few days that label would stick forever.

The Sh*t Just Hit The Fan - March 2023

Have you ever looked out in the distance and you could see dark clouds forming? You know a storm is on the way and there's nothing you can do about it. It's coming whether you're prepared for it or not. In the Old Testament of the Bible, God would often show up as a tornado and anyone who was foolish enough to challenge God would be destroyed. Needless to say God showed up as a tornado at this point in my life.

"Mr. Baldwin, I'm deputy Smith. Your wife has been placed under arrest."

I got the call out of the blue a week after I filed for divorce. Something straight out of a movie came into reality. You couldn't make it up, it felt so unreal.

Now I had threatened divorce twice already, but this time she knew I was serious. In the past she would often threaten suicide and cry her eyes out until I forgave her and tried to make the marriage work. When she saw the three thousand dollars withdrawn from the checking account and I told her I'm divorcing her she knew no amount of acting would change my course. So she flipped the script.

Out of spite for me filing for divorce she went to the local police station and filed an Emergency Protective Order (or EPO for short) against me. She knew the law and had every intention to hit me where it hurt the most: my children. My wife was in the county jail, my kids placed in custody of the state, and I was kicked out of my house and home, not able to see any of them until a court ordered hearing two weeks out. What happened?

There was a problem with Katie's EPO she never saw coming. When an EPO is signed by the judge, a deputy is sent out to serve you the paperwork. In the original EPO my wife said that the shotgun was missing and she was scared for her life. Now I remember telling her two weeks prior that I was placing the shotgun in the storage unit because I didn't want her to feel unsafe. I even recorded myself telling her in case I needed to use the recording in the future as evidence. I would no longer carry firearms in the home while I was divorcing my wife. However, in the EPO, I was homicidal and on the verge of killing her at any moment's notice.

The deputy and two social workers had gone out to my house to serve me with the EPO. However, when they got there, the three kids (ages 2, 3, and 5 at the time) were home alone. I was at work and Katie was no where to be found. When she finally showed back up at the house she used the excuse that she just went to go pick up McDonald's for the kids and was coming right back. Anyone that's worked with children know that you cannot do this. If you want to get food, you bring your kids with you.

"Mr. Baldwin, your wife has been charged with three counts of wanton child endangerment." Deputy Smith explained to me. "You are to come to the Edmondson social services office and sign your EPO."

My world fell apart. Out of spite my wife fabricated a false allegation against me and in the end it was her own sin that got her arrested for child neglect. The gallow she set for me was the same gallow that she got hung on.

Quickly I left work, called every close family member saying my wife had been arrested, and planned to meet with Kim, my mother-in-law, and Tyler, my brother-in-law, at my house and then to the social security office where they were holding my babies. We got to the house, I grabbed the children's car seats, and drove to the social security office with my work truck. Both Kim and Tyler followed close behind.

At the office I was sat down to be interrogated. You have to understand they only could go off what the EPO had said. I was a violent man and I was just as guilty as my wife for neglecting the children. Upon initial interrogation I was the bad guy. They looked seething as they were talking to me... until I got to explain myself and the situation. My wife had been cheating on me over the past year. I was the sole bread winner of the family. I had no idea my Katie was leaving them in the house by themselves (which would later be revealed she did this "all the time" according to her own words at a future court date). I felt bad for not knowing and wish I dug deeper, earlier in our marriage.

As I explained myself one of the women gave a sigh of empathy. She knew I was the one who was wronged, but she also knew I had to be held accountable to the EPO. "Mr. Baldwin, I'm here to serve you with this EPO." rang out Deputy Smith as he laid the papers in front of me. I read it. Katie had written that I was homicidal. A fabricated lie from a spiteful woman that I would have to fight against in the soon coming months. I agreed to have received the charges against me and signed the papers.

Signing the papers meant I would no longer be able to see my children until a court date two weeks out. I had no option in this matter. If I went against the court order and visited my kids without a judge granting me access I could get arrested and thrown into jail. I couldn't afford to lose that privilege so I would have to suck it up until the court date.

They asked me if I wanted to see the kids one last time before not seeing them again until I got the approval from the judge in two weeks. I shook my head vehemently, eyes wide, and said, "No. The kids would go crazy. Especially Maverick."

What no one knew was my kids desperately loved me. Their mother never did anything with them. She never played with them, never danced with them, never sung songs with them, nothing. Over the last two years she stayed locked in her room while I took care of the children whenever I was there. I loved them with all my heart and it showed. Every kid was a Daddy's boy/girl and they had grown a deep attachment for me. Their mother was jealous of their love for me and couldn't understand why. To me it was easy. I loved them hard, therefore they loved me hard.

With the decline of seeing my own kids I made an arrangement with their grandma, my mother-in-law, Kim. She would stay at my house and watch the kids while I would stay at her house and wait for the trial to see them again. It would prove the hardest emotional time in my entire forty years of my life. A time I finally understood just how much our Father in Heaven loves us. A fatherly love I never experienced and a deep longing to see my children again.

Because of Katie's arrest and three felony counts of wanton child endangerment she too was barred from seeing the children. If she didn't royally screw up, when they went to serve me with the EPO paperwork, she would have access to the house, children, vehicles, and I would be kicked to the curb as the bad guy in this story. I do believe it to be God working all things out for good for those who love Him that saved my butt that day and I'll be forever grateful for His mercy.

I handed my house key to Kim and wished her well. The children would be considered placed in foster care with Kim as the primary custodian. She would watch them in my house until I could find a replacement nanny. Everyone had tears in their eyes. The hard reality of life had just begun and the storm had just hit the shore. It was going to be a rough ride. I was in the fires of tribulation and Superman wasn't coming to save me.

ROCK BOTTOM

I like to look at this chapter of my life as my personal Book of Job. For those who don't know who Job was, he was a man of God who was put through trials and tribulations. God allowed the devil to have full reign on his body, his possessions, and even his family in order to test Job. By the end of the Book of Job, God had stripped Job of everything and yet Job refused to curse God. He knew God created him and he knew his life was at the mercy of God's judgment.

God has the power to kill you at any moment, but he allows you to live if there's still purpose in your life. As the Apostle Paul said he would rather be home with the Lord, but God still had a plan for his life. Therefore he allowed Paul to live until all his letters were fully written for the New Testament. The same for Job. By the end of the Book of Job, God not only replenished Job's possessions and children, but he doubled what he had throughout his second half of life.

That's where this story takes place. Rock bottom. No house. No children. No financial security. I literally lost everything and the next three months would prove the hardest time I've ever had in my entire life. I would be pushed mentally, emotionally, and financially to the brink of despair. All my past troubles would look as if it were a training ground all for this moment, this time, this place. My entire life was leading to this very chapter and it was just beginning. If it wasn't going to break me, it was going to make me stronger. I was not going to give up. I was not going to surrender. God was my refuge and I put my full trust in Him.

Because the EPO said the shotgun was missing, Deputy Smith had been assigned to confiscate my firearm until the EPO was dismissed. When you get an EPO filed against you, law enforcement is required to hold all your weapons and ammo until the judge releases you from the EPO. That means throughout the entirety of the EPO you can only defend yourself with your bare hands. Is that stupid? Partly. I can see it being effective against a really dangerous individual, but my wife fabricated the entire thing and I was at its mercy.

Smith walked me to my truck and noticed my registration tags were expired. I had been driving without insurance for a few months because we didn't have the finances in order at the time. No insurance? No registration. I was no longer allowed to drive it. To make matters worse, it would have to be towed. Great. The last thing you want is a bill from the tow company. Every day it sits in the yard is another $50 added to the bill. Time is against me. I have to act fast. I would have to get car insurance and then register my truck before I could even pull it out of the tow yard.

I was invited into his cop cruiser, only he let me ride shotgun. I found it funny. I was so polite with saying, "Yes, sir." And, "No, sir." And my demeaned was so nonthreatening that Deputy Smith was allowing me to ride with him in the front seat of his cruiser. I wasn't being treated like a villain, but someone who has been vilified by a spiteful woman. And Deputy Smith understood exactly what was happening.

I had put my shotgun into the storage unit and thought to myself I had told Katie specifically about it two weeks earlier. "Hey, I'm putting my shotgun in our storage unit because I don't want you to feel unsafe." I even recorded the audio (which I still have to this day) as evidence that I was putting it into the storage unit. For two whole weeks it was not in our house and yet in the EPO she said the shotgun was missing and she didn't know where it was. All a lie to get me kicked out of my house and home and it worked.

"Now John, I know what you're going through." Deputy Smith eluded. "I'm going to give you one advice. Listen to me clearly. Once this is all over and your EPO goes away, you get your house back, your kids back, and your shotgun back. You must never get back with this woman again. If, for whatever reason, she files another EPO against you, even if it's a lie, it's over. You will lose everything."

Deputy Smith had twenty years in the armed forces as a marine and going on close to thirty in the police force. I knew he was speaking from experience. He told me he went through the same thing with his ex and he's seen it happen to other men. I knew if, for whatever insane reason, I ever chose to get back with Katie, I would be risking losing my children again. Only this time it would be permanent. With that in mind I made the conscious decision to never remarry my wife for the rest of my life. Had she have never filed an EPO against me, there was still a glimmer of hope for remarriage. Deputy Smith nailed that coffin shut. Katie was now my enemy and I needed to severe our relationship completely.

We showed up at the storage, I took my shotgun out, and handed it to Deputy Smith. He unloaded the rounds, put it in his trunk, and we were off again to my house. During the ride back I was just asking for advice on my situation and what to do next. He gave me more good pointers and I was dropped off at my house. I was no longer allowed into the house itself. Not until the judge gave me a pass. I had worked out an arrangement with Kim where we would swap both houses and cars.

When they arrested my wife, they charged her with three felony counts of wanton child endangerment. Not only that, but she also got tacked on a misdemeanor charge for driving a car with expired registration stickers. When everything went down we were already stretched thin in finances. We were originally going to use the income tax returns to get everything caught up and everyone paid. However when I decided to divorce my wife I switched that as my primary focus. Now I was facing the financial difficulty of not only getting car insurance on my truck, register the truck, get the truck out of the impound, and also get insurance and registration on my SUV as well, without which no one could drive it.

Right before I left social services I swapped car keys with Kim. By the time Deputy Smith dropped me back off at the social services parking lot Kim and the kids were gone. She had taken them back to the house and I was not allowed to step within 500 ft of the house while they were in them or I risked being arrested and sent to jail. I couldn't let that happen as my finances would already be stretched thin. I couldn't miss a day at work. I got into Kim's car and started my drive to Kim's house.

While I drove there a lot of things went through my head. It was the first time I ever experienced true loneliness and despair. My children, my life blood, my seed... all removed from my life due to a spiteful woman bent on taking me down because I wanted to divorce her for cheating on me. All lies. Everything fabricated. And yet she was thrown in jail for abandoning our three young children alone in the house. For what? McDonald's? That's what she said, but I'll never know if that was really why she left them mid-day.

As I was driving to my new, temporary home I remembered Deputy Smith telling me a funny story that I could only think had to be an act of God. I was in the passenger side of his cruiser when he said to me, "John, in my thirty years of law enforcement I've never served an EPO only to end up arresting the file complainant." I smirked.

Scorched Earth

"I want you to live like no one else. Go scorched earth on your debt. Sell so much stuff that the kids think they're next." - Dave Ramsey

I first caught on to Dave Ramsey's program about a decade ago, but I never really put it into practice. A primary reason was my wife was the spender in the family while I was the saver. Having lived through this type of marriage made me realize I should have vetted better before deciding to marry her. I've also come to realize if you're potential future spouse is not good with money being single, they won't magically change into a money guru the minute they say, "I do." Vet wisely, men.

The first step, in Dave Ramsey's baby steps, is to save a baby emergency fund of one thousand dollars. I remember always having an emergency all the time. We had tried to save up even a few hundred dollars over the years, but were never successful. There was always an emergency. However, looking back on my time spent with my wife, I still remember her say distinctly, "We will never be rich! There's no point in saving!"

What people don't understand about government subsidies is they penalize you for being smart with your money. If they give you give hundred dollars cash for food stamps, if you don't use it up they will lower your allotted monthly stipend. Not only that, but nothing rolls over. You have to use it that month. What's worse is if you save over two thousand dollars in a savings or retirement account they will stop paying you.

Jasher had a monthly government assistance check that was being deposited into a debit card. He was officially diagnosed with autism a few years back and we had been collecting approximately eight hundred dollars a month that was supposed to be used for his continued well-being. Unfortunately the card was not in my possession and Katie had put the legal guardianship of the money in her name. I never thought much about it until now.

I came to realize she knew the system. Her plan was to get all three children on disability as well as food stamps and live off that. Jasher was diagnosed with autism, but Katie wanted to file the other two as having a disability as well. Maverick was rowdy all the time and unruly. Jubilee would constantly rock herself and scream. She couldn't be left alone in a room by herself or she would go insane.

It would dawn on me, after everything was all over a year later, that none of the kids were really autistic, they were neglected. Even from a baby I was the sole nurturer in their lives. I would pick them up, play with them, caress them, sing to them, dance with them, and just love on them. Meanwhile Katie would lock herself up in the room for hours, never seeing her own babies. By the end of our marriage I would always come home to a destroyed house and children who were so happy to see me as if they had no one throughout the day.

I learned that, as Katie stayed in her room, Maverick would destroy the house. The reason why was because he figured any attention was better than no attention. As long as Mommy stayed locked in her room for hours Maverick would be making loud noises and causing trouble in the hopes of his mother simply coming out and recognizing him. He was starving for affection and he would get attention even if it meant he would make Mommy angry.

And poor Jubilee. She was only two years old at the time. All she could do was scream and cry. Katie would often send me messages throughout the day saying, "These kids are horrible, John! They wrecked the house and you're going to clean it! I'm going back to bed!" Jubilee needed a nurturing mother figure more than anyone else. To this day she is hooked on any attention from a female. She's desperately trying to fill the feminine void her mother never showed. It's one reason both Kim and I agree as to why Jubilee's hair never really grew until she was out of that situation. Too much stress.

And now my biggest emergency was at hand. No house, but I still had to pay the mortgage to keep it from falling into foreclosure, two vehicles that needed insurance and registration, and one in the impound that would go up every single day. That's not including food, gas, and figuring out the babysitting issue at hand. Kim offered to help, but couldn't stay away from work for more than two weeks. She was banking on the judge letting me back into the house sometime soon. Needless to say I was stretched thin and the money I had put aside into savings was going to dry up real fast.

Every penny counted. Every penny mattered. I would have to go scorched Earth to achieve the unachievable. I would have to be extra strict on my budget. Budget? I had no budget. I would have to start one. Dave Ramsey's baby steps. That Unfortunately baby step one would continue to elude me over the course of the next six months. I couldn't save up for an emergency, I was in it!

Rock Bottom

Two weeks was a long time to wait to see my kids again. Up to this point I thought I had felt emotional pain, but nothing would come close to this. I've never gone more than a day or two without seeing my kids. They couldn't live without me. And now I was out of their lives without an understanding of where I was. I broke down. Every single day I cried for them. I missed them. I loved them. With all my heart.

A new emotion came over me that day. Something I never experienced in all my life. Fatherly love. True fatherly love. For the first time I looked at the pictures of my son and all I felt was compassion, joy, and misery all at the same time. I loved them so much and I couldn't see them. I was bound by the laws of the land, imprisoned by a spiteful woman. For the first time ever I understood the love God has for His children and it was a sacrificial love. I would proudly lay down my life for these little ones and I knew more than ever I had to continue to fight.

Maverick suffered the most. He just didn't understand. I was his every-thing. To this day he's extremely close to me. Always wanting to sit in my lap and sleep next to me, but during this time of absence he was struggling. It was the longest he's ever gone without me. Kim would tell me he would break down and cry out to me, always running to the window to see if I would be pulling up in the drive way. She would tell him I was busy working and it wouldn't be long until I came back. Jasher and Jubilee were still hurting, but he was definitely hurting the most out of everyone.

I had made an arrangement with Britany, a family friend who had babysat for us in the past. She would act as live-in nanny and watch them full time while I was away. I drew up a contract and within the first week she would replace Kim as caretaker and Kim would be free to return back to her house. By this time I had gotten both vehicles insured and registered as well as getting my truck out of the impound. It costed me nearly a thousand dollars to get everything situated. That was a huge strain on my finances.

I worked out an agreement with Britany to have her use my SUV while I used her car. It was cheaper on gas than driving my truck everywhere for visitation and she could use the SUV to drive the kids to the grocery or anywhere she needed to be. The courts granted me two hours per day to see the children. I decided I would use my time to tuck the kids in bed every night before driving back to Brittany's place to crash. That way I could work full time, drive to her place, change clothes and shower, drive back to my house to tuck them in at night, and drive back to Brittany's and reset for the day.

It would end up going like that for the next forty days and forty nights. That's how long I would end up having to wait for the entire EPO to be dropped. In the entirety of the forty days, I distinctly remember only missing one or two days because I had medical appointments during those times. If it weren't for those, I was there every day. I couldn't live without them, they were like a breath of fresh air every time I saw them. They really enjoyed me tucking them in at night as the last person they saw before going to bed. Bedtime story, prayer, hug, and kiss goodnight.

Final Sacrifices

Eventually money became too tight with, not only paying for the live-in nanny, but all the gas, utilities, and food. I was running out of funds so I started donating plasma for $50 a week. To me it was a symbol of my undying sacrifice just to continue to see them. Literal blood, sweat, and tears in order to pay for gas just to see them every day. I also stopped eating as much in order to save money for gas and continue paying for their food. I lost fifteen pounds during the forty days, all due to food restriction and stress.

The last week of the forty days arrived and I was yet again out of money. Music was my only escape. I would often continue to practice on the piano at my house and at Britany's. There was one musical instrument that I swore I would pass on for generations as an heirloom, my Celtic harp. It was the first instrument I ever purchased and my most prized possession. It was in storage and one of my most expensive items of value. I looked at my money and looked at my gas. One quarter of a tank left. I needed more gas.

I thought a lot of how much that harp meant to me. It was like an extension of myself, my spirit, my being. I saved an entire paycheck for it and paid for professional harp lessons. I saw myself a master harpist in thirty years, but over time it had collected dust. I fell in love with the piano. I started playing the piano religiously over the last year and a half before everything went to crap. I had gotten pretty good and it became my means of escape during this turmoil.

I listed the harp for sale on Facebook marketplace and got a prospective buyer, but she was only able to budget $250 for it. I had originally bought it for $650 and, depending on the market, they can go all the way up to $1200. I paused, looked at the harp, looked at my gas, thought of the kids. "They're worth it. Lord, you got me this far. I'm willing to sacrifice everything for them. They're worth it."

With tears in my eyes I told the girl a short story of my current situation and how long I've had the harp for. She was in her twenty's and traveled out of state just to buy the harp. She was enjoyed at the idea of playing the harp and I could tell it meant the world to her. For me the $250 meant the world to me. It meant I could get more gas and pay for my last few meals before court next week. I handed over the harp, collected my money, and wished her the best.

I then drove to the local gas station to fill up. Full tank. I put the rest in my billfold, I would have to pay the nanny and save some for food, for myself and for the babies. Driving to my house brought a tear to my eye. I was willing to sacrifice everything, all my worldly goods, for the ones I loved most. It would all be worth it in the end. They were my everything, my gifts from God and I loved them with all my heart. They were worth it.

God Will Provide A Lamb Sacrifice

Genesis 22:6-8 KJV — And Abraham took the wood of the burnt offering, and laid it upon Isaac his son; and he took the fire in his hand, and a knife; and they went both of them together. And Isaac spake unto Abraham his father, and said, My father: and he said, Here am I, my son. And he said, Behold the fire and the wood: but where is the lamb for a burnt offering? And Abraham said, My son, God will provide himself a lamb for a burnt offering: so they went both of them together.

Through this time I had gone through a lot of ups and downs. I had sacrificed a lot and I was willing to sacrifice everything. I had been tested and I persevered to the end. I didn't give up my faith and I wasn't going to quit. I was determined to come out the winner. The words came to me as if I could see them clear as day: "God Will Provide Himself A Lamb Sacrifice"

I had never thought about it like that before. From my time of study to practice I had always thought you had to do something to get something in return. Sure, I had been saved many years ago, but the idea of God providing His own sacrifice for Himself never really resonated with me until now. I had been completely dependent on hope and a prayer for these past forty days and was seeing, with my own eyes, the blessings of God's love.

The fact my wife set up gallows for me, but was hung on her own gallows by getting arrested while I rode in the passenger side of Deputy Smith's cruiser. The fact I was able to financially take care of two household's at the same time, Brittany's and myself, and still see the kids every single day. The fact the judge extended my hours to two hours per day and I was able to tuck the kids in every night. The fact I was able to sell my harp as soon as I posted it for sale which supported both my gas and my food for the last week of my EPO. It was like a hand was guiding me all along, a hand that loved me and would make sure I would be okay throughout this entire event, God's hand.

God was very much real in my life and I was a living example of a miracle. God had sustained me and was providing for Himself a lamb sacrifice. I didn't have to provide anything, He provided it all for me. And now my forty days and forty nights were coming to a close. Tomorrow was my court day where I would have to defend myself and see if they would drop the EPO or if it would continue. I couldn't keep this up, I was barely hanging on and had little money left in my checking account.

Judgment Day - May 2023

Forty days and forty nights. I counted them up from beginning to end. My eyes lit up. The number forty has spiritual meaning behind it. The flood of Noah lasted forty days and forty nights. Jesus went into the wilderness, to be tempted of Satan the devil, for forty days and forty nights. And here I was, in court, on the fortieth day. The EPO was served to me at night so that made forty days and forty nights exact. Was my EPO going to be extended or was it going to be dissolved and I get my house, my cars, and my shotgun back? Today was judgment day.

My lawyer was sitting next to me and Katie was across the room. I remember watching the Johnny Depp trial and how he vowed never to look at her again. I understood why. I felt the same. I couldn't look at her. Throughout this entire time I had been accused of being a dangerous man, that I was homicidal, and that my wife was in danger. She fraudulently filed the EPO in spite of me filing for divorce and she wasn't getting punished. My accuser was the manipulator and the abuser and yet I was the one being punished.

"Mr. Baldwin, why did you act hysterical and say you were homicidal?" My lawyer asked me before the court.

"Because she kept cheating on me." I responded with tears in my eyes.

My lawyer made the argument I was emotionally distraught at the time after finding my wife cheating on me for a fifth time. The prosecution tried to argue against it saying it had no merit as I had said I was homicidal when it all came down. They were referencing a 911 call I had placed where I told dispatch to send a deputy out because I was homicidal. I was planning on taking my shotgun and driving out to the man's house and shooting him. I had his phone number, his address, and I had the intent to kill... until I talked to the officer.

The sheriff had pulled up to my driveway at the time. I was sitting on my front porch, breaking down in tears over my wife cheating on me yet again and feeling stuck. With his words of encouragement he was able to change my mind and calm me down. I had to take control of myself for the sake of my children and I needed to divorce this woman. That was before my wife ever got arrested, but it was bring brought to the court's table as evidence of me being a dangerous man.

"Why did you say you were homicidal, Mr. Baldwin?" Katie's lawyer inquired.

"Because I was in the military and I've been trained to always call someone anytime anyone mentions suicide or homicide." I responded.

It was true. My motives were simple. The fact I was even saying I was homicidal out loud was enough for my years of training to kick in. I was in the U.S. Navy for five years and the Texas Army National Guard for two. We were trained to always report anyone immediately who said they had thoughts of suicide or homicide. I was having a panic attack and still had the whereabouts to call 911 the second those words left my mouth. Deep down inside I didn't want to kill anyone, yet at that moment I was feeling rage and I knew I had to talk to someone.

My lawyer went back and forth with her lawyer, defending each other's case. The whole time I couldn't look at my wife, I just wanted my children back. My house, my home, my life. I hardly said a word. Katie, on the other hand, was very belligerent. It was easy to see she was angry and vindictive. Angry I would dare divorce her. Angry I would fight back. She wanted to continue the EPO for the sole purpose of hurting me. There was no other reason. She knew I was a great father, but because I said she was a bad mother she was determined to make me suffer.

"Mrs. Baldwin," the judge responded to Katie in closing. "I don't think you're afraid of any man. When Mr. Baldwin was homicidal it was him that called for help, not you. An Emergency Protective Order states that the accused will be held accountable for such crimes if found to have abuse, drug addiction, or stalking. My conclusion is Mr. Baldwin is not at fault. Therefore I am dissolving this EPO immediately."

I broke down in tears. My lawyer told me to breathe. That I had won. I had been wonderfully accused and I had been set free. Free to see my children again, free to live in my house again, and free to protect myself again with my shotgun. I had made it. I had been restored. I had won.

The War's Not Over

I had fought the battle and won, but the war wasn't over. I had won my EPO trial, but the kids still belonged to the state. They would be placed under my supervision, in my house, but under the state's control until the divorce was finalized. After proving I was an innocent man, wrongfully accused by a spiteful woman, I was still having to pay the penalty for the state becoming involved in my family affairs. It wasn't right, it wasn't fair, but the world isn't fair.

"Time to suck it up, buttercup! These kids need me!" I said to myself.

I didn't drive home yet. There was still one last thing I needed to do before reuniting with my family again.

"Yes, I'm here to pick up my shotgun." I told the woman at the dispatch window. Ten minutes of waiting later one of the deputies came out from behind the door with my shotgun. A sense of freedom came over me. It was my right to protect myself and my family. During the last forty days and forty nights there was no way to protect my own children and I wasn't around to help defend against them. Now my right to bare arms was being returned to me as a symbol of the victory I faced in court.

The deputy spoke to me confidently. I had a feeling the place knew about my court appearance. As if Deputy Smith had been keeping them informed of the irresponsible behavior my wife had put me through. Perhaps it was all a part of my imagination and I was just living in the high of it all. I was still beaming with joy that I was able to beat my own enemy. The person who took me to court over fabricated lies was hung on her own gallows she had built for me. It felt good.

I drove home and gave all my kids a big hug. I told them I was no longer going to be gone and I would stay with them forever. The only one that understood it was Jasher and he was really happy. Eventually everyone went back to their houses. Kim drove back to hers as did Britany, but she would help me in the near future. I still had the issue of the mortgage approaching foreclosure. I had to work fast.

I got in touch with a real estate agent and we put it on the market. It was still in rather damaged shape and I didn't have the money to recondition the place so I did the best with what I could. Within one week a prospective buyer was serious so it was go time. I had to move everything out of the house like it was yesterday. With Britany's help I was able to move all my house possessions to a local storage unit. With that I signed the papers and took my check.

The house sold for a profit of $32,000. Split evenly, Katie took $18k and I took the other $18k. I moved into a double wide trailer for just $650 a month. It had work that needed to make it liveable so with $2k I was able to buy three window AC units, a fridge, and other needed appliances. That left me with $16k. I still owed my sister and a few others close to $2k because I told them I would pay them back when the house sold. $14k left. I thought to myself I really couldn't have done it without Kim's help so I gifted Kim $1000. $13k remained.

Last was Britany. She was my biggest help. Not only did she go above and beyond the call of duty of watching my kids, but I still owed her roughly $1000 in back pay. But I wanted to show my true appreciation for her. Without her I couldn't have done it. Watching my kids, helping me clean the house to sell it, help transfer my possessions into a local storage unit... I decided I would reward her with $10,000. Total $11k to her left me with $2k. $18,000 down to $2000. That would be the money that could sustain me for the next few months for food and utilities, I figured. Fair trade for being grateful to the ones who were there for you when you needed them the most.

When God Speaks, You Listen - June 2023

I knew God called me to music about a year before I ever met my wife. I had just laid down in bed when my eyes were filled with white light and an overwhelming sense of joy came over me. Now my eyes were still shut, but inside them all I could see is light. Then a voice came to me as if by audibly speaking in my ear, "I want you to write new hymns."

"How can this be, Lord? When I don't know how to play any musical instruments?" I responded.

"I will bless your hands and your memory so you may learn quickly." I heard back.

"How many hymns do you want me to write?" I asked confidently, this time supposing it really was the Lord and not just a dream.

"Until I tell you to stop."

And then the voice stopped and the light went away and I opened my eyes and the room was dark. I just was in disbelief at what I had experienced. Perhaps it was just a figment of my own imagination.

I fought this idea over the next month. I wrestled with God telling Him he had the wrong guy. At this point in my life I had only sung in choir and music teams. I didn't know how to play an instrument. God chose poorly. I wasn't his man. But I was. At the end of one month and the overwhelming conviction to play music for Him I gave in and said, "Lord, if it is your will that I play music for you, I will to it with all my might. I surrender to you, Lord. I will be your musician."

From there I bought my first musical instrument, the harp. It was my pride and joy and I got music lessons within the first month of purchase. Eventually I sold it to that girl I told you about earlier in order to have enough money to pay for gas during the last week of my EPO. The kids were worth more to me than any musical instrument.

A few months later, as promised, new songs were popping into my head left and right. Almost a new song every day. I had to write them down. Then I figured if I had to write them, I might as well learn how to play them with a guitar, so I got a cheap guitar for $50. I thought no one else could play the songs like I wanted them to sound so I put all my songs to music. Because of my professional harp lessons, the music learning carried on to any stringed instrument so I learned how to play the guitar in about two months and I would eventually get pretty good after three years.

I woke up one morning with a song in my head. Almost audible. I had to write it down, it was an insatiable desire to put this song to music. It was the weekend so I wrote it down, put it to music, and uploaded it to YouTube. Little did I know, exactly one year from that upload, my first born son would be born into this world. Jasher Baldwin, born June 15, 2017. "Still Learning", my song, uploaded June 14, 2016. It's still on YouTube to this day.

Fast forward to today, we had just moved into the new place and I had an insatiable desire to buy a digital piano. Problem was I didn't have enough resources. The budget digital piano was $500 and if I were to buy it, it would send me into a financial hole. Deep down inside I knew I had to purchase it though. Music was really God's calling on my life and I knew, if He wanted me to buy a budget digital piano, He would provide the resources necessary. The words "God will provide Himself a lamb sacrifice" kept resonating in my head over and over again. With the faith of a mustard seed I made the decision to purchase the digital piano.

It was light enough to carry around the house wherever I needed it to be and operated in a way that I would never have to worry about tuning it. It was an investment that could be very well played for the next ten years and so to me it was a great investment in my continued growth in music practice. If God really called me into music, He would provide the financial means to make it a reality, right?

The very next day I got a letter in the mail. I had no idea about this, but when your house sells they also give you an equity check later on if you have excess equity built into your mortgage. We had lived in the house for three years and it had built up a bit of equity. It was an equity check for $1200. Above and beyond what I needed to not only purchase the digital piano, but also pay for more of my groceries and utilities. I knew God saw my faith and my trust in Him that day. I knew God would provide a Himself a lamb sacrifice. I just didn't know it would be the very next day. God is good.

Word of caution to the reader: Remember to only do this when you know 100% certain that it's God's calling in your life. To do so otherwise would tempt God and be foolish on your behalf. Do not take God's blessings for granted. If God isn't calling you into something, don't spend the finances before the provision. God called me into music. Find out God's calling in your life before you take a leap of faith.

Kindergarten - August 2023

This is where we started. Jasher was finally going into kindergarten at the age of six. At the start of this journey of infidelity into divorce filings into EPO into getting kicked out of my own house Jasher was still in diapers. He was five years old and still in diapers. Katie never tried to teach him to be potty trained. It was Britany the live-in nanny that finally guided him into toilet training and he was fully potty trained by his sixth birthday. Now he was attending kindergarten.

My story isn't done just yet. The EPO was cleared and my housing situation was cleared, but there was still the divorce that had to be finalized. I was still receiving monthly visitations from the state. It was over the course of the next year that I discovered balance in the chaos. I was able to bring stability to what seemed like an impossible emotional roller-coaster. I was near the finish line, but it wasn't over yet. However I was quickly learning what was necessary to become the best parent that I could be for my tribe, my children, my life.

In the chapters to come I will go over the most important skills necessary to achieve success with your family. The loyalty you experience and the joy it brings. The sense of honor when you hear others compliment on how well behaved your children are, how clean they are, and how respectful they are to others. They're all sweet kids, but I believe it's achievable for anyone who wants it bad enough and is willing to do whatever it takes to become the Greatest Dad On Planet Earth.

SECTION II

How I Became The Greatest Dad On Planet Earth

CHILDCARE

As a single father the hardest challenge, I ever had, centered around childcare. This specific area of parenting would be the biggest learning curve of my entire adult life. The sheer thought of the unknown was the only thing standing between me and fully divorcing my wife. I had no idea what I was going to do. Over the last six years my wife was a stay-at-home mom. I went to work and brought home the bacon while my wife stayed at home and watched the kids. Not anymore.

I was determined to make it work no matter what. I had no experience in child rearing outside of my time spent with them after work or on the weekends. I had no concept of hiring a babysitter let alone child healthcare. Since the kids were born, Katie was always in charge of their medical needs. If they needed to be taken to the doctor she would take them with the family SUV. She would fill out all their medical documentation online.

Needless to say I had a lot to learn. It was intimidating. One minute you're hardly involved in the children's day to day activities, the next you bare full responsibility. Are you going to sink or swim? Most people would think it irresponsible of me for not knowing my own children's medical information. However this is how we agreed at the start of our relationship. Katie would handle all the medical needs of the children while I focused on bringing home an income to support all of them. It worked until the burden was shifted over to me.

This would be the defining line that would set me on the path to becoming a great father. What do you do when you have no one? You still have to get to work and your children still have to be clothed, fed, and looked after while you're gone. You're going to need help from someone and you're going to have to make it work no matter what. Child care is going to be your biggest hurdle, but once you master it, it becomes like second hand nature to you.

Get a Babysitter

Britany quit. No two weeks notice, no heads up, she just quit cold turkey. I had given her the $10,000 the week prior and now she was gone. Kim told me she was just waiting for the money before heading out. Kim was right. It was a growing suspicion that Britany would leave as soon as I gave her the bonus and that's exactly what she did.

I can't blame her though. She had worked as my live-in nanny over the last three months. She didn't get one vacation day in. She had to stay at the house day in and day out. She was burned out and had enough of me and the children. Not that she had any hate towards any of us, but she wanted to get back to her normal life again and I couldn't blame her. I was on her side and I fully understood.

The only problem lied in the fact I had a new problem now. Who would be the new babysitter? The house was finally sold. I had finally moved to the new place with kids in tow. Britany had her own family she had to take care of. She was now gone and I was left desperate for help. "Sink or swim, John. Time to swim."

People had been following me on Facebook for some time, following my story as it was unraveling. Several people knew of my wife's infidelity and arrest. I had to reach out to my community and ask for help. I was in desperate need of a babysitter. I made a post on my page asking for help and help arrived in the form of a Facebook group. Someone referred me to join the babysitter group of Bowling Green so I did.

A few hours went by and I was approved to join the group. Desperate for help I made a post telling a brief story of my situation. I had no one and needed a babysitter. Not only that, but I couldn't afford much. I attached one family photo of the kids so any potential babysitters could see what they looked like. I submitted the post for approval and waited.

Within a few minutes my post was approved and I was getting messages left and right from women who were willing to work with me. They were willing to help. I felt desperate and started to make a list of willing participants to watch my children. First I had to make sure they were close enough to drive to and drop off. Next I had to make sure they were in my budget. $25 a child per day is what I could afford. It wasn't much, but these women were willing to help me. Some of them said they understood what I was going through.

With that I had three babysitters in rotation. Some days one of them would be sick so I would reach out to the other two. Other days they would have medical appointments with their own children. I found out, rather quickly, that relying on one person to watch your children was a bad idea. During the time Britany was my live-in nanny I was still under the mindset of her acting as a mother to my children. I realized I was wrong for this and it wasn't right to put her in that situation. Had I hired other babysitters to rotate with Britany, there was a chance she wouldn't have been burned out and quit out of the blue.

It was a hard lesson for me that will stick with me until the day I die. Rule #1 when it comes to babysitters: Have multiple babysitters in rotation. By the time I've written this book it's been two years since this happened. I've had my children go through many different babysitters during this time. Some women dropped off the babysitting game completely. Some I still work with to this day. Moral of the story is never burn any bridges. You'll never know when you'll need someone to watch your kids at the last second.

Pay Up Front

I looked around at the people around me. A lot of them looked desperate, but so was I. In a way this was a reminder to me, a question if you will. Are you willing to do whatever it takes? I was. And this was proof of it.

A needle was stuck in my arm and a long tube, attached to a machine, was pumping my blood. Every few minutes it would reverse rotation and blood, and saline, would flow back into my arm. I was donating plasma for cash. While I may have had the funds necessary to pay Britany, the babysitter, my paychecks weren't enough to cover the cost of both her vehicle and mine. When I drew out the nanny agreement I also put in there that I would cover the cost of her gas and all the food. After all, she was watching my babies full time and had no other income to support her driving them to doctor's appointments.

To make ends meet I was not only selling stuff in the house that I no longer needed, but also donating plasma for cash. During my EPO I was allotted two hours each day to see my children. I was so desperate to see them that I would drive to the house every day and spend my two hours playing with them and catching up with Britany to see if I needed to buy more groceries or make sure she had the gas to go and purchase the groceries for me. Gas had become my biggest liability at the time and unless I did something drastic I wouldn't have the funds necessary to support continued visitation.

So there I was... in a chair... with a needle stuck in my arm donating plasma. They allowed you to donate every four days with a maximum of twice per week. It was initially $200 to be a new donar and $100 max per week, $50 per session after that. All in all I made roughly $700 through donating plasma until he sale of the house. This would ensure I not only had the funds necessary to pay my babysitter off, but to continue supporting the basic needs of taking care of my children while I was away.

Rule #2 when it comes to babysitters: Always pay the babysitter first. These are your children. They're worth taking care of. Make sure your babysitter(s) are happy. If they're happy, they will reciprocate that happiness onto your children. If they're not happy, your children will suffer in the process. Will the babysitter neglect your children if you don't pay? We would like to think not. However remember that your babysitters are humans too. They have a rent or mortgage payment as well. If they're stressed out because they're not being paid on time, how do you think that stress will be reflected onto your children?

I remember reading a story, on the Facebook babysitter group, where a woman had conned another woman out of $300 worth of child care. She told her she was going to pay her the following week, but when the following week came the woman was no where to be found. That's two weeks of child care given basically for free and now that woman can no longer post on the babysitting group for help with her children. She, in essence, screwed herself over.

When I pay up front the babysitters are generally taken off guard. Most of their clients are other women. I am the exception to the rule. I pay up front on dropping off my children. I look at it as they're going to use the money to feed my children while I'm at work. Some of these women don't have that many things, often living paycheck to paycheck. When you pay up front, you relieve some of the burden attached to basic child care necessities like food and the electric bill that heats the home your child will be staying at. Be considerate and always pay up front. Do whatever it takes if your children are really worth it.

Bring A Diaper Bag

"I put her extra clothes and a snack in the diaper bag. There's also medicine in the side pocket." I told the babysitter while I dropped off Jubilee.

Early on I learned to always pack an extra set of clothes for your babies. That and medicine. You never knew when the kids would make a mess or get sick. For the babysitter this was crucial. I remember the first time I started testing new babysitters. I would get a message saying Jubilee had an accident and, thankfully, the babysitter had another change of clothes. I would wash them and bring them back. I didn't like the idea of my daughter having to wear another girl's clothes so I quickly changed my strategy.

I picked an outfit, Jubilee didn't wear as much, and placed it in a Ziploc bag. Then I placed the bag into the diaper bag I had purchased off Amazon. It would be an essential tool in my arsenal of childcare essentials. I also prepared a snack for Jubilee to eat. I knew the babysitter would provide lunch, but some babysitters wouldn't be as generous as others. You have to think about it. I'm paying $30/day. That's not including meals. These babysitters are really getting the short end of the stick when it comes to child care and finances.

Last was medicine. During the first year of the kids finally being in school, it felt like the kids kept getting sick week after week. One week one would get strep throat. The next week the other would catch it and the following the other would catch it. Then one got the flu and next thing you know the other two start showing symptoms the following two weeks. It was like this for four straight months where I would lose a day at work at least once a week or every two weeks. Thankfully my employer was willing to work with me because I was such a great worker and they didn't want to lose me. My personal work ethic and devotion was the only thing that kept me from getting fired. That and a great boss.

When your kids get sick, you keep them home, give them medicine, and hope they make a full recovery. That's great under a two parent household. Each parent can take turns watching the kids while the other continues to bring home the bacon. Not so easy under a one parent household. You have to get clever. Before taking my children to a babysitter's house, I had to warn them ahead of time and request if it were okay to bring them over. Sometimes, as long as they didn't run a fever, they were okay with watching the kids. Other times it was a flat out no. That's where juggling different babysitters became extremely effective.

Take a Ziploc bag and put Ibuprofen and Tylenol in it. Place it in the diaper bag and make sure your babysitter knows it's in there. I always put a measuring syringe in there as well so the babysitter will just have to miss out on work. I hope you have PTO stocked up for this very occasion. However, for the cases another person can watch them without fear of them being too contagious, keep medicine in your diaper bag.

Vet Carefully

Proverbs 11:14 KJV — Where no counsel is, the people fall: but in the multitude of counsellors there is safety.

Desperate times call for desperate measures. When you have nobody and little money, you'll take whatever you can get. The following will elaborate on the old saying, "You get what you pay for."

In the beginning I had no choice. I was up against a wall and had to take the first woman who would be willing to watch my kids. Britany had quit. I had no one. I still had to work and the kids still had to be watched. I was able to low ball budget a babysitter for $25/hr. I thought to myself, "Thank God." Little did I know this would end up being an ill adventure.

The first babysitter I had ended up being a woman in her thirties with a great reputation of sending me daily photos of the kids while I was at work. Problem was her house always smelled heavily of marijuana. I knew I was dropping the children off at her place and they would be exposed to second hand marijuana smoke, but I really had no choice at the time. She was able to work with me on payments and I paid her at the end of the week, cold hard cash. I kept the kids with her for about two months until August came around and I was able to take Jasher into kindergarten, Maverick and Jubilee into daycare.

The second babysitter was a woman in her early twenties. She was living with her mom at the time and boyfriend. Same price, different problems. This one Jasher said he didn't want to go to, but never told me why. He would remain quiet when I pressed him for information so I became concerned. I started to think maybe it was because she wasn't feeding him the foods he wanted or maybe he didn't get along with the other kids under her watch. Whatever it was, he wasn't telling me so I felt I needed to move to another babysitter.

A number of months, after Jasher started school, I put out a help wanted post on the Babysitters Facebook page. A young twenty year old woman responded she could help and I agreed to it. Unfortunately, when I got to her location, she had pulled a switcheroo on me and had her mom watch Jasher. Now I always visit the babysitter ahead of time to check out their place. This is a good habit. It was a single-wide trailer home with all new furnishings. She just started renting there. Even though she switched me to her mom, we exchanged numbers and I started having the bus drop Jasher off at her place and I would come over, after work, to pick him up.

I then received a call from Kim, my mother-in-law. She had received word that Jasher was being dropped off at a place that had an anarchist truck parked in the front yard. Turns out the bus driver was so concerned he decided to report it to my network of people on Jasher's safe list and I became concerned as well. Turns out her mother's boyfriend looked like something straight out of a skin head gang.

I pulled up and saw him throwing something into his white pick-up truck. His head was completely shaven off, tattoos all over, goatee, and rugged attire. His truck matched his tattoos with marks all over, anarchist symbols and other symbols I could not recognize. Immediately my red flags were going off. "I've got to get my son out of here." I thought to myself. Some would have frowned upon me for letting my son stay a few more days, but I had no one else at the time so I told her it would only be until Friday. She agreed and I was able to pick my son up until I got him situated with another babysitter.

There were many other babysitters along the way, but the tide turned in my favor when I was finally able to afford $30/day. Well what do you know? Turns out the higher I was willing to pay these babysitters the higher quality babysitters I got. Eventually I was able to work my way up to $40/day and I had the very best babysitters in the white collar suburbs. Depending on your budget and your area your experience may defer, but I've learned that what you pay for is really what you get. And if you're willing to pay for higher value babysitters, you can really become The Greatest Dad On Planet Earth.

CREATURES OF HABIT

"What are you doing son?" I asked Jasher, currently three years old at the time.

Jasher didn't say anything. He just laughed. He was putting his toy miniature dinosaurs in a row on the floor. They were all in a line. Jasher often did this with any of his toys. He was diagnosed with autism at an early age, but I could tell he was different from birth. Even though he was my first child, looking back at all my children I can definitely tell that Jasher was different. He was special. He acted different, he was a picky eater, and he interacted with others differently as well. A very loving boy at that.

One thing that stuck out to me was how he would cry and throw a fit if things were out of order. If we were spending the night somewhere else he would cry. He had to have everything a specific way. A way of life and routine that wasn't chaotic. Even with his dinosaurs in a line, it was an outward expression of his desire to keep things in order. While Maverick and Jubilee didn't mind a mess, Jasher had to have the toys in a neat line or order of arrangement.

During my marriage I thought nothing of this. My wife agreed to be a stay-at-home mom and watch the kids while I was at work so it was her responsibility to do a majority of the house work. That included giving the kids proper baths, folding their clothes, and making their meals. Unfortunately Katie was not like that. When we first got married she agreed to these terms and would be a homemaker. In reality I was just the golden ticket to an easy life, one of which she would just have to kick her feet up and take it easy, sleeping through most of the day and playing games and social media on her phone throughout the night.

Thus my kids' would suffer. There was no organization, no routine, no guidance while I was at work, nothing. Eventually all three of our children would develop behavioral developmental issues primarily onset by child neglect. And while one could argue I was the head of the household. Why didn't I do more? The problem was I couldn't. I had a full time job. As the sole breadwinner of the family, it was my responsibility to bring home the bacon and watch the children after I got home from work. And with limited time until they were put to bed, I only had a 2 - 3 hour window to do anything for the kids outside of the weekends.

By the end of our marriage I was doing all the household chores while Katie slept in most days and stayed up through most of the night. I even told her that was the reason why she wasn't getting up early and taking care of the kids. Because how can someone watch the kids during the day if they stay up throughout the night? No one can do that. I found myself coming home from work to change all the babies' diapers, do all the dishes, wipe down all the countertops, sweep the floors, mop the floors, take out the trash, and do the laundry. I often felt like I was the only one trying in our marriage. And I was.

Routine, Routine, Routine

One of the most developing habits I've learned is my kids thrive on routine. Reduced chaos and set schedules have been the biggest life hack I've ever done. It's amazing that I never did anything like I do today when I was married, but how much better my life would have been had I only developed these basic routines at the start of my fatherhood. I will go over a typical Mon - Fri, from wake up to sleep.

03:30 - Wake up. Pray over my kids. Start exercise routine.

04:10 - Take a cold shower. Brush teeth. Get dressed for work.

04:20 - Practice piano.

05:00 - Start morning routine. Fix my breakfast and lunch. Pack the kids' snack bags. Put everything in the car. Get the kids' tooth brushes ready.

06:00 - Wake kids up. Tell them good morning and I love them. Get them dressed. Brush their teeth. Get them in the car.

06:30 - Head out to drop kids off.

06:50 - Drop Maverick off at daycare.

07:00 - Drop Jasher & Jubilee off at school. Head to work.

07:30 - Arrive at work.

08:00 - Start working.

16:30 - Finish working. Head off to pick the boys up.

17:00 - Pick Jasher up from The Core.

17:15 - Pick Maverick up from Little Sprouts Daycare. Head home.

18:00 - Arrive home. Jubilee is dropped off by my neighbor.

18:30 - Start making dinner.

19:00 - Give the kids dinner. Start eating dinner.

20:00 - Give the kids a bath. Brush their teeth.

20:30 - Read kids a book. Say their prayers with them. Tuck them into bed, tell them I love them and say good night.

21:00 - Clean dishes, sweep floor, throw out trash, put all the toys away, pick clothes for kids and lay them on the couch for tomorrow.

21:30 - Finish any miscellaneous projects or personal errands. Watch a portion of a movie. Play a game. Whatever I feel like doing that's fun and is a break from the rigid schedule. A time to relax.

22:00 - Take a shower & prepare clothes for tomorrow. Start winding down.

22:30 - Pray over my kids one more time. Go to bed. This gives me exactly five hours of sleep. Time to reset and start all over in the morning.

Some would think, "This rigidity is insane. Who would do this? Five hours of sleep isn't enough. I can't live with this schedule." You would be right in your thinking process. Most people cannot be this disciplined to live by a strict schedule. Life happens and we can't all stick to a format like this.

However what I gave you was an example. It's what I had to do in order for my life to be put in order. I don't have another person to drop the kids off at school. That's my job. I don't have anyone else making dinner for the kids. If I don't continue to improve on myself through exercise and hobby, I'll get burned out. I need some form of stress relief that can improve my overall well-being. For me that's exercise and piano. Unfortunately I only have so much time throughout the week. It requires me to wake up extra early just so I can get these two needs met.

Whatever a normal day looks like for you, is there structure? Are you putting your kids to bed at a specific time each day or are you putting them in bed whenever you get the time for it? Does their life have some form of structure, some form of discipline, or is it more chaotic? Do your children eat whenever and whatever they want? Do they stay hooked on television or a tablet throughout the day when they get home from school? Are they able to play without any electronic entertainment for over an hour?

In the beginning it was very hard. While I was married I came home and took care of the kids and did all the house chores. My wife, at the time, made dinner every night. I'll give her that. But the time to put the kids to bed was random. They also took baths few and far in between. They didn't have a set time for brushing their teeth and going to sleep. I didn't pay attention to their needs as much as I do now. How could I? I only had so much time after work to spend with the kids and pick up their mess. I was relying on my wife to set their schedule accordingly.

Well I was wrong. I should have stepped up, but when you're in the first all you see are the trees. Now I know better. Now I have set time frames established and a routine built into their hardware. They now get hungry at the same time, sleepy at the same time, and are less irritable when they wake up in the morning. They get roughly ten hours of sleep each night and their moods have improved. When I snapped to reality, in the beginning of my divorce proceedings, I saw the heavy bags around their eyes. Those have long gone and their health has improved exponentially since then.

Rest & Recovery

Genesis 2:2-3 KJV — And on the seventh day God ended his work which he had made; and he rested on the seventh day from all his work which he had made. And God blessed the seventh day, and sanctified it: because that in it he had rested from all his work which God created and made.

Mark 2:27 KJV — And he said unto them, The sabbath was made for man, and not man for the sabbath:

As I told my son, in the previous chapter, there are three things that are necessary to building muscle: exercise, meat, and rest. Exercise to stimulate the muscle, meat for the protein needed to build the muscle, and rest for the time needed for muscle to recover and rebuild itself stronger than before. Muscle is built during the rest, not the exercise.

As we were created in God's image, why do some people believe they don't need a rest day when even God Almighty took a whole day to rest from His work? God knew what He was doing when He made the Sabbath. He worked hard for 6 days and on the 7th day, He rested. He took time off His busy schedule and scheduled a planned vacation. A time to relax and reflect on what He built. He created the entire world you see around you and all the creatures that live in it including man. And then He rested.

I started celebrating the physical Sabbath about twenty years ago. While I'm not Jewish, I took the scripture to heart and started implementing it into my own life. What I found out was it opened my world to what real rest and recovery looked like and how much family time can benefit my entire tribe. Not only was it beneficial to myself, but my children as well. When I was single, I used this day as a time to recharge my batteries. I would sleep in late, practice my music, watch movies, go on dates, all with zero regret or guilt.

Once I had children my views on the Sabbath shifted and I understood the benefits for the entire family. A full day of rest and relaxation to enjoy with the entire family. Sounds like a vacation, doesn't it? That's because it is. It's a time to sleep in with your kids, a time to go to the park together, a time to bond with one another. I've developed a routine where every Saturday we go to the park. Kids wake me up around 7 am and I make them breakfast. Around 10 am we're on the road heading to the park and around noon we head out to grab a bite to eat and get groceries. They look forward to it every Saturday.

Family Before Church

1 Timothy 5:8 KJV — But if any provide not for his own, and specially for those of his own house, he hath denied the faith, and is worse than an infidel.

Quality time is one of the greatest things you can give to your children. They desire your love. They desire your time. They desire you. You are their everything. They need you. So many parents live their lives focused on their careers so much their children get put on the back burner. I've even seen some "christian households" place their church above their own families. Some denominations even encourage it. This is the wrong approach.

God created man before man created religion. It is important that we treat our own household with more appreciation before treating the church we go to as priority. I'm an analytical person. I work well with a set of guidelines to follow, it keeps me in check. It holds myself accountable. I've learned this is the proper structure to follow and always in this order: God, Family, Community

No one is above God, not even yourself. Not your family; not your church; God. God is #1. Always and forever. With saying that, the Bible is clear that if you love God you will keep His commandments. The ten commandments is a set of guidelines that allow us to see the world through a moral compass. There are rules to follow and there are consequences for disobeying those rules. I'm sure everyone can agree that murder is bad, but it was only a few thousand years ago that tribes were still engaging in cannibalism. Thus there had to be a written law somewhere, a golden set of rules to help mankind. Those golden rules were the ten commandments.

Children are no different. They need rules to be governed. What is right? What is wrong? The ten commandments simplifies this for you. Commandment number one eludes to the fact that God is always number one. Therefore, if He is number one, His commandments are to be obeyed above all else. Commandment number five states that children are to honor their parents. This is something that has weakened over time in Western culture. America has less respect for the nuclear family than what the Bible teaches. And the sixth commandment is to not murder. It saddens me that this needs to be written down, but unfortunately some people need to read it and obey.

Once you align yourself with God's laws and take an effort to following them, your family will passively benefit. Your moral compass will fall into place and you can rightfully teach right from wrong. Your children can gain guidance on, not only the nature of God's judgement, but the hope of the eternal to come. God's laws transcend human laws and give purpose to those without direction. It is a foundation that will help guide your children into contributing to the wellness of society as a whole.

Once you family is in order, then comes community. This includes the church. Too often members get burned out by either the people, the message, or the duties. If the people are toxic, move. If the message is toxic, move. If your duties are too burdensome, get help. Church must never take precedence over your family and your family must never take precedence over God. If your family is sick, you won't be well in the church. Make sure your community never becomes more important than your family.

With the order of how your tribe should function, given the priority of most important to least, you must always look to keep some form of structure in your household. The foundation should always be God first, family second, community third. Pray first thing in the morning, pray last thing at night. Feed, clothe, and protect your family and keep close relations to those who care about your eternal being. You're not alone in this world. There are genuine people who care about you that are willing to stand the gap and help when you are down. What better place than to look in your local church?

Personal Finance

"If you can live like no one else, later you can live and give like no one else."
- Dave Ramsey

"Say cheese!" I exclaimed as I held up my camera phone. I had the kids on the couch sitting next to each other. They were all very happy to receive their very first piggy bank. By this point we had fully settled into the new place and their extended family was sending them money laid inside birthday cards. Every birthday and Christmas there would be money to be given to the kids and I currently had an envelope system where I put their money in envelopes in my safe.

I wanted the kids to start getting a grasp on how money works. In order to do this I had to make sure they could touch, feel, and access their money at any point in time. While they were just children and savings had no bearing on their understanding, it was important to me to get them started in the right direction. Having them understand it takes money to buy things and there's a limit to how much they can buy was crucial in their financial development.

They all smiled as I took a picture. It had been raining outside and Jubilee still had her rain boots on; the boys, socks. They each held their piggy banks in their hands. I had bought three different colors to sepa-rate each child and they each picked their own color. Jasher got a red piggy bank, Maverick got blue, and Jubilee got yellow. I took a picture of them and made it into my Facebook banner. Originally my Facebook was about my marriage with Katie, but after she left I had full control and changed it to a page devoted just for them. I wanted their extended family to see I was putting them on a great path financially.

Personal finance starts with you. If your finances are in chaos, so will be your household. Everything starts with a budget. If you don't know where your money is going, at the end of the month, stop and evaluate your spending. As of recent studies, around 36% of Americans would struggle to cover a $1,000 emergency expense with cash, savings, or a credit card paid off within a month. This statistic comes from surveys like those conducted by Bankrate and aligns with longstanding financial stress trends in the U.S. It highlights that a significant portion of the population relies on borrowing or alternative sources to handle unexpected costs.

One of my biggest financial influences has been a man named Dave Ramsey. For those, who have never heard of him, Dave Ramsey is a personal finance expert, author, and radio host known for promoting debt-free living and financial independence. He created the "7 Baby Steps" framework, emphasizing budgeting, saving for emergencies, and investing. He's helped millions improve their financial health and achieve financial freedom.

The primary driver, in motivating me to create a budget and live by it, has been Dave Ramsey's guidance. During my time of struggle I was forced to get pay day loans and borrow from family until my house sold, at which point I paid everyone back. During this time I had no budget, no game plan, no outlook on life. I had to liquidate my retirement just to be able to keep my house out of foreclosure and get it sold. Because of the constant emphasis on having a budget I was finally able to get my finances in order and live within my means long after my divorce was finalized. Now I'm on my way to retiring with dignity.

Financial stress is inevitable. Everyone will go through some form of it sometime in their life whether it deal with a couple bucks or millions of dollars. Without a written game plan, there is no purpose, no meaning, no direction. It is important that every man gets his personal finances together before he gets his children's. Your tribe needs to look at you as the leader physically, emotionally, spiritually, and financially. They depend on your financial well-being and you need a written game plan in order to contribute to society rather than being a burden to it.

While Dave Ramsey isn't for everyone, he's just an example. There are many other financial gurus and professionals that can help you achieve financial freedom. However, in most cases, the basic foundation stays the same: have a written budget, save up cash for an emergency, pay off bad debt, and invest in your retirement. There are other goals you can add to this list, but this is the bare bones of financial responsibility. It is important that every man make some sort of strive to ensure all these things are taken care of before you get too old to work. You don't want to end up old with no nest egg. You've worked way too hard to end up with nothing. Change your financial trajectory today!

Plenty of Discipline, Lots of Love

"Good morning, son! I love you!"

I got Jasher out of bed. Jasher was now in a routine of getting up for school. I would always get him up first. It was Monday again. It was always hardest on Mondays after a full two day weekend. Everyone had to reset.

"Today I go to school, Dad?" Jasher asked inquisitively.

"You know this son." I responded.

"I'm going to Kindergarten?" He responded back.

"Yes, son. I love you." Jasher gave me a hug, eyes still half asleep. I gave him a kiss.

I made myself a social experiment to see what would happen if I told my kids I loved them a thousand times and hugged and kissed them a thousand more? How would they turn out?

When I was a child my father was an abusive alcoholic. Every day he would drink and every day he would call us "little shits." While it seemed harmless at the time, it would play a crucial role in my development. In my early adulthood I was afraid of becoming like my father. I didn't want to become an alcoholic as he was. I didn't want to call my children curse words. My father's abuse showed me what not to be and I made a valiant effort to be a different man.

Before I ever got married I made a vow, to myself, to never drink in front of any of my children. While I do drink on special occasions such as dinner dates, weddings, festivals, etc, to this day not one of my children have ever seen me drink a drop of alcohol. Because of my own father's alcoholism I was able to see a potential side of me I never wanted to come to fruition. Therefore I chose not to carry on that negative DNA and cut it at the roots.

Before I ever got married I spent two whole years to clean up my language. I would take careful thought into the words that left my mouth before speaking them into existence. I made a valiant effort to not speak one single curse word with the sole purpose of never letting any of my children hear a single swear word come out of my mouth. To this day all my hard work has paid off. My children live in a house that's both alcohol free and curse free. If they ever start swearing, they didn't learn it from me.

Aggressive Love

I still remember the day my son was born. I couldn't stand the sight of blood so I chose to hold my wife's hand instead. She pushed and eventually he popped out. Jasher Harold Baldwin. I named him after a prophet in the Bible, the lost Book of Jasher. The name Jasher appears only twice in the entire text. His middle name I named after my father-in-law, Katie's father, Harold Gaw. In a way I thought of the song, "Hark the Harold Angel sing. Glory to the newborn king." I hummed it in my head the day he was born.

Out of paranoia I remember digging through my old baby pictures and finding my earliest one. I had been born in the Philippines on American soil. My dad was in the U.S. Navy at the time when he met my mom and I was born on a U.S. Naval base. My dad was white and my mom was Filipina. My wife was white so Jasher came out three quarters white. I had seen the youngest photo of myself on a passport. I was a pretty fat baby. As soon as Jasher came out of the womb I saw his face and it looked like an exact copy of my photo as a baby. No need for a DNA test, this boy was mine. It was one of the greatest achievements in my life, having that boy. I had always wanted kids even as a teenager.

I sat with Jasher in our living room. Jasher was just a few days old. Mom was sleeping in the bedroom getting rested up from her delivery. It was just me and my boy. I looked at him. He looked at me. I was in love. I made a vow then and there to always take care of him even if it costed me my own life. "My life before yours." I told him if I ever had to sacrifice myself. I would die before he ever did. My soul was bound to his for life and I had to ensure he lived passed me. I was thirty-two years old at the time.

Over time I found an interesting correlation that should be well known, but isn't practiced in a lot of households including the one I grew up in as a child. The energy you put into a relationship will be the same energy you get out of the relationship. If you put negative energy into a relationship, don't be surprised if you get negative energy back. If you put positive energy into a relationship, don't be surprised if you get positive energy back.

My father was an abusive alcoholic. When I became a teenager I made the conscious decision to stop giving my dad hugs and kisses. I didn't feel loved by him, so I would stop trying. I still remember it being years into my adulthood when I finally forgave my dad and gave him a hug. He was caught off guard. I hadn't given him a hug for almost a decade. My childhood played a big role in the type of man I would eventually become.

I made the conscious decision that I would tell my kids I loved them every single day and give them hugs and kisses throughout the day. From the moment I wake them up, I tell them I love them. When I tuck them into bed at night, I tell them I love them. Every time I drop them off at school, I tell them I love them. When I pick them back up, I tell them I love them. You get the picture. I must tell them I love them about a hundred times each day and it shows with my children coming up to me, at random times throughout the day, and telling me, "I love you, Dad!"

I also made the conscious decision to give my kids hundreds of kisses, hugs, and tickles. It's as if their love tank is always full when they're around me. They'll often come up to me and want a hug. I never deny them. I've come to realize that's how they feel loved. When Daddy gives them a hug they feel safe and loved. At any point in time, if they ask for a hug, kiss, tickle, or being picked up I satisfy that need immediately. I don't delay it. I know it will make them feel loved and their moods will remain high.

If your child ever wants affection of any kind, give it to them immediately. Not only that, but be aggressive. Proactively hug and kiss your child. When they're not looking, pounce on them and smother them with love. Chase after them and act like you're a monster about to eat them. They love that as they run away and laugh. Tickle them with extreme aggression, giving breaks every few seconds for them to catch their breath. If you want them to feel loved, love them hard and love them with intent.

Love Tanks

"Inside every child is an 'emotional tank' waiting to be filled with love. When a child really feels loved, he will develop normally, but when the love tank is empty, the child will misbehave. Much of the misbehavior of children is motivated by the cravings of an empty 'love tank.'" - Gary Chapman, *The 5 Love Languages*

As I explained in earlier chapters, when my son, Maverick, was still a toddler he would destroy the house every time I was gone to work. His mother would lock herself in her room all day and only come out to feed them and maybe change them one time throughout the entire day. She neglected his basic needs so much I would often come home to his diaper in one room and his poop in another. That's right, he would often defecate on the floor after his diaper was too heavy and would fall off his bottom.

Maverick's love language is physical touch. I've noticed he is most happy whenever he gets hugs, kisses, picked up, thrown around, and always wants me to carry him or sit on my lap. He thrives on physical touch. His mother hardly carried him even as a baby. I would do the majority of touching because my love language is physical touch as well. Maverick naturally fell in love with me because we both filled each other's love tanks.

Maverick would only lash out in anger while I was at work. He would only destroy the house when I was gone. Whenever I was there he was an angel and desired to always hang out with me. He wanted to be anything Daddy was and would want to spend every waking hour with me, but I wasn't there. I was at work. Why did he destroy everything when I wasn't present? Because negative attention is better than no attention at all.

As said before, his mother would lock herself in her room most of the day, only to come out to feed the kids or change them once or twice. That was his only connection with his mother. She didn't like carrying the kids so he would be left to himself, often crying. In anger he would turn to destroy the house when the hopes that his mother would come out and pick him up. Maybe she would play with him. Instead she would come out, take pictures of the destruction, and send them to me with the caption, "These kids are bad, John!"

Every child has a love tank. Find out which love language your child enjoys and try to compliment that as much as possible. Every child is different so you'll have to figure it out yourself. But when you do find out their language, be aggressive with giving that type of love so their love tank remains full at all times.

Spare The Rod, Spoil The Child

Proverbs 13:24 KJV — He that spareth his rod hateth his son: but he that loveth him chasteneth him betimes.

"Fire! Fire! Fire!" I yelled out at my dad. I was seven years old at the time. I was a bit of a pyromaniac, I loved to play with fire. We lived out in the boonies of Arkansas and my dad would burn the trash in a metal barrel. Everyone was inside, watching TV or playing. I was outside, admiring the fire.

For whatever crazy idea I had, I thought it would be fun to light a small tree branch on fire, bring it to the property line, and throw it on the leaves to start another fire. It certainly did light up and I was suddenly taken back with the reality of what I just did. The small fire I started was picking up speed and fast. I started to stomp on the fire to no avail. I had no idea what to do so I ran inside the house and cried to my father who instantly jumped out of his seat and ran outside.

My father had one leg and a prosthetic attachment. He couldn't run fast. He had lost his left leg in a motorcycle accident before I was ever born. They had to amputate it off before it could catch gang green so I've only ever known my father with one leg. Well he certainly ran out as fast as he could with a prosthetic to grab the water hose and spray the fire down. By the time he reached it the fire had started to engulf the barbed wire fence line and part of the neighbor's backyard.

I ran to the bathroom window and looked outside. Everyone was standing around my dad as he was drenching the flames with the garden hose. I was the only one inside the house. My dad turned his head towards the house and his eyes locked with mine. I knew the gig was up. No way to lie about this one. I was the only one not in the group. Guilty as charged. As my dad put out the last of the flames I could start to hear the beating of my heartbeat. I knew this wasn't going to end well. I went into the living room and awaited my fate. My dad stepped into the room with Mom, brother, and two sisters close behind them.

"John, why did you start a fire?" My dad asked, voice loud and stern.

I didn't know what to say. At the time it seemed cool to play with fire and I wanted to light something else on fire. "I just wanted to see." I whimpered.

"The neighbor is an old lady! You could have burned her up in it!" My dad yelled back.

The idea never hit me that I could have killed somebody. I was only seven years old, I never thought about the repercussions of my actions that far out. I never thought things all the way through, I just did them. I liked playing with fire and wanted to start a new one is all I could think about. Well my father wasn't pleased with my desire to experiment and he would make sure I learned my lesson for the rest of my life.

What followed would have to be the hardest spanking I ever received in my entire life. It's as if my father grew a metal lining around his hand and wanted to make me feel the very life force leave my body. From the moment I was born until today's present day, I have never been spanked as hard as I had been that day. It's as if my father's own hand had turned into a wooden paddle and whopped me into the fourth dimension of reality. Time and space stopped as my butt caved in for what seemed like an eternity.

I ran to my room and shut the door as I fell down in pain and misery. All I could think about was how I just wanted to play with the fire and how badly my butt hurt. It was a new reality and a new me. I would be a good boy from then on.

I never played with fire after that. I also remember that day as the most painful butt whooping in human history. I also think to myself, "I deserved that." every time I look back at that spanking. If I ever desserved a spanking in my entire life, that was the one moment I did. There was a chance I could have started a fire in the neighbor's woods and killed her in the process. That butt whooping was well deserved and I often use it as a reference for why discipline works.

I find it interesting that today's culture has gotten a little soft around parenting. A lot of parents want to be their child's best friend. While this may seem harmless on the outside, you're doing your child a disservice. Your child isn't your friend. He or she is your son or daughter. There must be an emotional separation of the two mindsets. They cannot coexist.

No.

"I don't want to take a bath! I'll just go to bed, Dad!" Maverick told me.

"No." I responded back. "You're taking a bath."

"I don't want to take a bath! I'll just go to bed!" Maverick screamed louder.

"No, Maverick. You're taking a bath." I raised my voice slightly. Maverick was my biggest no child. Out of the three, he was the hardest to deal with. He would stubbornly come as close to the line as possible when it dealt with boundaries. This time was no different. Maverick was sleepy. He didn't want a bath. Unfortunately he was dirty and I wasn't about to have him go to bed in filth. He was going to take a bath whether he liked it or not.

This is one of many examples that have happened over the course of my time alone with the kids. Once I had full custody I had to be the judge and executioner of every decision for these little ones. I didn't have another mediator to decide their basic needs and wants, it was all on my hands. I had to get them ready for school every day, I had to cook and clean up after them, and I had to ensure their health was the best it could be. I had to assume the role of leader and provider of the household. As leader, Maverick was taking a bath.

Few words come close to the power in saying the word, "No." Especially in today's culture, the world is full of yes men. Too many people say yes. Not enough men say no. Too many people are worried about what others will think than to stand up to themselves and tell the world no. I believe it is more important today to have a backbone and stand firm on your feet. If you don't like something, say no. If someone wants to hang out with you, but you don't have the time, tell them no. Anytime you don't feel right about any situation, do not say yes until you are 100% confident it's the right move. Until then, say no.

Children test you. I've seen many parents get run over by their own children because they want to be their best friend. This is not the right mentality to have. By saying yes to your child every time they scream, you are displaying weakness and they will grow up to become ungrateful little brats. There is power in the word no. The more you use it, the more power you have in your own household and the more of a leader you will look in the eyes of your children.

Jasher was the easiest child. I never had to spank him much. If I told him to do something, he would. A part of me feels very conflicted about this. A boy, who does not display any argumentive qualities growing up, can end up a yes man when they get older. This is not good for self confidence. It is good if you have a child that is easy to deal with, but when they become an adult you don't want them to be a pushover. You want them to develop a strong balance between saying yes and saying no. Agreeability and argumentive.

Maverick would eventually get a pop in the butt. It is important to not show any sign of wavering to your children. When you lay ground rules down, the children are to follow it with zero exceptions. When you tell your child to do something, they better do it or face your wrath as their executioner. You aren't their friend, you're their father. Now act like it. If they ask to do something, and you say no and they start to cry, tell them no one more time and then lay down the law.

My father used to count to three. If I were in trouble he would start with, "One... two..." At that point I was scared and did as he said. I feel this is not the right way to discipline your children. There should be no countdown. You make the laws of your house and you ensure they follow them. You give one warning and, if they continue to disobey, you discipline them. They need to realize there are consequences for their actions and you are serious. The minute they step out of line, passed the initial warning you gave, you are to discipline them.

Balance

Yin and Yang is a fundamental concept in Chinese philosophy and culture that represents the dual nature of reality. It describes how seemingly opposite forces are interconnected and interdependent in the natural world. Yin is associated with qualities such as darkness, passivity, femininity, and receptivity, while Yang embodies light, activity, masculinity, and assertiveness. The interplay between these two forces creates balance and harmony in life. The famous symbol of Yin and Yang, a circle divided into black (Yin) and white (Yang) sections, illustrates this balance, suggesting that within each force lies a seed of the other. The concept emphasizes the importance of balance in all aspects of life, suggesting that harmony arises from the interplay of opposing elements.

I like to think of love as Yin and discipline as Yang. While I consider myself a Bible believing Christian, this representation still holds true in parenting. There must be a balance. Too much love and you create ungrateful, selfish, entitled little brats. Too much discipline and you create resentful, abusive, hardened little twits. Neither of which you want as grown adults. Remember you're raising little humans. You want them to contribute to society, not be a burden to it.

As I've stated before, my father was an abusive alcoholic. He would often yell at us for any reason. I remember, one time as a child, I was simply standing in the middle of the kitchen talking to him and he would yell at me to move. Had he not been drunk at the time he could have easily told me to move without yelling at me or gently placed his hand on me to move me out of the way. It's a technique I've learned to do with my children. If they're in the way, place one or two hands gently on the child and carefully move them by hand. It let's them know you recognize they're there and guides them out of the way.

There's no perfect way to raise a child. Everyone's situation is different. Every child is different. Our teaching habits are usually influenced somewhat from our upbringing. The key takeaway is that these children will be grown adults one day. We are to raise them to contribute to society, not be a burden to it. Aggressively love your children. Find out what their specific love languages are and tailor how you show your love to those languages. And above all, discipline their little behinds when they get out of line. Do these things and they will feel a balanced, genuine appreciation for them that they'll reciprocate back to you in the present and when you're gray haired in the years to come.

I Want To Be Strong

"Look at my muscles, Dad!"

Jasher flexed his arms in a strongman pose. He curled his arms in the air with pride as he looked at me for affirmation.

"I want to be strong!"

"You have to eat meat, son." I responded back.

Jasher was my pickiest eater. Every since he was a baby Jasher had always avoided meat other than chicken nuggets at McDonald's. I was determined not to have any of my children eat McDonald's every week as they had when I was still living with Katie. Under my household my children's diets were much better.

"Jasher, do you know what builds muscle?" I asked.

"Uh uh." Jasher shrugged in question.

"Three things: exercise, meat, and rest. If you don't have those three things, you won't build muscle."

Jasher nodded in agreement, but he had no idea what I was talking about. His focus was to get strong. How he would get there? By flexing his muscles more. I simply told him that I loved him. He loved me back.

10 Push-ups a Day

Encouraged by Jasher's determination to get stronger I decided it would be a good idea to implement a new strategy. 10 Push-ups a day. Jasher was only seven. Maverick was four. I've been in and out of the gym over the last twenty years and there's one thing that has stuck with me through it all: Consistency.

More than proper form and physical prowess, consistency is the number one factor that separates the haves from the have nots. Without consistency there's no workout program on Earth that can make you stronger. No diet on Earth that can make you thinner. No education on Earth that can make you smarter. Consistency is the number one factor that will make you into a winner.

I made a new rule.

"Sons of Thunder!" I exclaimed. The boys had my attention. "From now on we will do ten push-ups every day when we come home from school. I'm going to make you strong!"

Jasher was excited. Maverick was excited to simply do something with Daddy. Every time Daddy would do something, Maverick had to join as well. Maverick wanted to be just like Daddy. If Daddy was doing pushups, Maverick would do push-ups as will.

"Front leaning rest position!" I yelled out as I went into a push-up stance, hands on the floor and my body in a plank. Just like my days in Army boot camp. "This is called the front leaning rest position."

The boys copied my stance on the floor.

"Down!"

I lowered my body to the floor. The boys followed suit. I rested on the floor until they stopped moving.

"Up! One!"

The boys pushed themselves up, butt in the air with an arched back. I didn't criticize their figure. It was more important for them to start getting into a habit of doing push-ups every day. I would correct their form in the future when they got stronger.

"Down!"

I lowered my body to the floor again and waited for the boys to copy my movements. Down they went.

"Up! Two!"

The boys' figures were very uncoordinated. They had no idea how to do a proper push-up. That didn't matter. What mattered the most was my boys were following in sync with me. With every push, they went up. With every drop, they went to the floor. Jubilee thought it fun so she started copying my movements as well.

"Down! Up! Three! Down! Up! Four!"

We went to ten. I was excited for the boys. They looked tired.

"Good job! High five!"

I gave them all high fives. It was important for them to get positive affirmation for this achievement. I decided to go above and beyond when it came to congratulating them on a job well done.

"Who wants chocolate?!" I asked out loud.

"Me! Me! Me! Chocolate!" They all shouted at once. I kept a bag of chocolates in the freezer so they wouldn't melt. I was using them to reward Maverick and Jubilee if they used the potty. Every time they used the potty they would get chocolate. Well this time they were getting chocolate for completing their first ever ten push-ups in a row! And they were happy. My goal was to show the correlation between hard work and reward. If we work really hard at something and finish it to the end, we get rewarded. In this case, chocolate.

Be Superman

By the time this book gets published I'll be forty years old. I look around and realize I'm in the minority. I'm in great shape. I graduated high school as the skinniest kid in my entire class. In fact, when I first started working out at age 18, my physical fitness trainer told me I was weaker than where I should be. Some people would get offended at that statement, but I was motivated. I knew he was just being honest and it motivated me to get stronger. Over the course of the last twenty years, going in and out of the gym, I've managed to add on thirty pounds of lean muscle mass. Sure, my muscle building genetics are pretty crappy, but I've always tried to maintain some form of physical activity.

Twenty years later and I find it a little depressing that I'm usually the fittest person in the room. Sure that's good for my self-confidence, but I find it sad that the vast majority of Americans tend to let themselves go after the age of 20. And, if anything, since the start of my divorce I've been motivated even further to get back into shape and go above and beyond. I'm currently 135+ lbs and my goal weight 165+. The first thirty pounds took me twenty years to put on. I'm so confident with my self-accountability that I know I can get the next thirty over the next ten years.

Your children need to see you as a strong father figure, not a weak slob. You bet your hard earned money your children are comparing you to other dads. What do you think happens when I show up to pick up my son, Jasher? Yes, he runs to to me and gives me a hug and kiss in public, but I see the other kids and they see me. I still give my kids piggyback rides every time I drop them off anywhere and pick them up. The other kids notice it. Their parents aren't doing that. Other parents are out of shape. Not me.

If you're out of shape, fitness needs to be priority. You want to be a great contribution to your children's lives, not a burden to them. If you can't pick up your own children and hold them for more than five minutes, you need to get in shape. There should be no reason you can't give piggyback rides to your children if they're still at a young age. For patients with older children, work out with your kids. I just told you I do ten push-ups with my kids every day. I still do that to this day.

It is important you become the leader you were meant to be. You are the head of the household. Your kids look up to you. They want to see you as Superman, not Water Boy. How can you lead your family if you're weak? Physical strength doesn't stay on your muscles, it effects everything. When you feel strong, you feel confident. When you feel confident, your attitude is better, your leading skills are better, and your children respect you more. Be strong because your kids need you to be strong. Be the Superman that saves your family, not the slob that drags them down.

Piggyback Rides

Milo of Croton was an ancient Greek wrestler and strongman from the city of Croton in southern Italy. Renowned for his incredible strength, he won numerous victories in the Olympic Games and other major athletic festivals in the 6th century BCE. Milo's training regimen, often associated with progressive overload, involved carrying a calf daily as it grew into a full-grown bull. His reputation extended beyond athletics, as he also played a key role in defending Croton from its enemies. Milo's life ended tragically when he was trapped by a fallen tree while trying to tear it apart.

Milo of Croton is famously associated with the idea of carrying a calf daily to build strength as it gradually grew into a bull. This practice demonstrated his belief in progressive overload, where gradually increasing weight helps muscles adapt and grow stronger. The story illustrates the importance of consistent, incremental training to achieve remarkable physical strength.

Out of all the physical activities, piggyback rides deserves a special place in the things you can do for your child that will almost never grow old and will keep you accountable to your own strength as you both grow older. Limited by possible physical disabilities you may have or your child is simply too old, if your children are young and you can carry their weight like a backpack, give them piggyback rides. As they grow older, you'll start to notice they'll actually feel lighter. As long as you're giving them piggyback rides every single day, you'll inherently get stronger just like Milo of Croton did with the calf.

"Dad!" Jasher yelled out when he saw me.

"Ready to go, son?" I responded.

"Yeah!"

I squated down, back straight, facing away from my boy. He jumped onto my back, arms around my neck. I jumped up, adjusting my shirt. I was picking him up from his after school program at The Core. It was like a YMCA that had fun activities for the kids to do while working parents, such as myself, could arrive later in the day to pick them up. Today was just like any other day.

"Ready, set, go!" Jasher called out. I then ran down the hall at a moderate speed as he laughed and held on for dear life. Of course, he was never in harms way. I crossed my arms behind my back and inter-locked them under his butt so he could sit comfortably while I ran. I also leaned forward slightly as to keep his center of balance directly on my back. For him it was the time of his life. He loved it every time I gave him a piggyback ride. For me it was a reminder I was still in shape and could sustain even a young boy on my back while I ran.

As Jasher grew bigger I noticed something strange that made me go, "hmm..." I noticed he felt lighter. All three of my children did. They just kept feeling lighter the older they got. At first I didn't think anything of it, but I even started noticing subtle changes in my own body even though I had not been in the gym in a few years. My triceps were getting bigger. Even my quads on my legs appeared to be growing. I had given piggyback rides consistently each day for his entire life, just out of love for the boy. And from this simple exercise I was growing more muscle.

If you can give piggyback rides, do it. It not only holds your own phys-ical health accountable, but it will be an encouragement to you as you get older. By the time this book gets published I'll be forty years old. While I've been in and out of the gym over the last twenty years, I can confidently say that piggyback rides have helped maintain my overall strength and lean muscle mass while providing love to my children. After all, every child loves a piggyback ride. Be the strong Daddy your kids can look up to.

Nutrition

During the divorce process I dropped 10-20 lbs. I was underweight. I just wasn't eating that much. I was so stressed out that I lost all my appetite. Slowly I have regained my hunger and I'm back eating at full capacity and making progress to strips my previous record of 146 lbs. I'm 5'9" and have always struggled with gaining weight. I graduated high school at 110 lbs, same height, the skinniest guy in my entire class. Over the course of the last twenty years I managed to put on thirty pounds from when I first started going to the gym.

While my case is rare, it isn't unique. The vast majority of Americans are overweight. But here lies the problem. No one is tracking their macros. People THINK they know how many calories they're consuming, but unless you're tracking them how can you be sure? You can't. Unless you track them every single day you cannot be one hundred percent certain if you're getting the appropriate calories to gain weight or staying under to lose weight.

"Calories in, calories out" (CICO) refers to the balance between the calories you consume through food and drink (calories in) and the calories your body uses for basic functions and physical activity (calories out). If you consume more calories than you burn, you gain weight; if you burn more calories than you consume, you lose weight. It's the basic concept behind weight management, emphasizing that the energy balance determines weight changes.

Now some studies have shown that CICO doesn't work and it can simply be a hormone issue. Some people even get defensive if you mention CICO, stating they tried it in the past, but it didn't work for them. When I question them about it, they don't have proof of tracking anything. What I find happens a lot of times is someone will track one day of eating and then stop, believing they'll keep eating at that level. Unfortunately calorie tracking doesn't work that way. If you're not tracking your calories every day, how can you really be sure? Simple answer is you won't.

The first thing I recommend is downloading a macro tracking app. I personally use Cronometer and track my foods every day outside of Saturday, my cheat day. Because my goal is to gain weight, I need to consume 4000+ calories every single day. My maintenance caloric intake sits close to 2500 calories. I'm pushing my caloric intake up 1000+ calories passed what's necessary to maintain my current weight.

Even with all the data, there are people who still believe CICO doesn't work. Most people just want an easy pill to swallow that will melt the fat off their bones with little to no work. In comes a pill called Ozempic. Ozempic is a prescription medication used to manage type 2 diabetes and support weight loss. It contains semaglutide, a GLP-1 receptor agonist, which helps regulate blood sugar by stimulating insulin production and reducing appetite. It's typically administered as a once-weekly injection. While it can aid in weight loss, it's primarily prescribed for blood sugar control, and its use for weight loss alone should be done under medical supervision.

Funny how this one pill makes you lose weight by controlling your hunger. Guess what happens when you are less hungry? You eat less. You're consuming less calories. Calories in, calories out. Even a magic weight loss drug makes you lose weight by limiting the amount of calories you intake in a day. People will say the pill works, but it's because it's making your brain think it's not that hungry, therefore you don't eat as much. CICO wins.

But what should you eat? While veganism has taken off for being a diet that can make you lose a lot of weight, the reality is the people are simply drinking more water and stop eating processed foods. Whole food diets remove the consumption of fast foods off your pallet. That alone improves your quality of health overall simply from eating less calorie packed food that comes in fast food. You also remove so much sugar water from your diet from all those sodas. I believe the first step, to good nutrition, is to stop eating fast food on a regular basis and start drinking more water. Water is life. Drink more water.

Second, eat meat. Or eat more of it. Again, my vegan readers will have a difficult time digesting this one, but hear me out. The body needs protein in order to heal itself and the best way to get protein is by eating meat. The absorption rate, or bioavailability, of red meat protein generally has a high absorption rate, ranging from about 90% to 99%. Animal proteins, including red meat, are considered complete proteins, meaning they contain all essential amino acids in proportions easily utilized by the body. Red meat has high bioavailability due to the presence of all essential amino acids and its similarity to human muscle tissue. This makes it easier for the body to break down and absorb.

Meanwhile plant-based proteins have a lower absorption rate, generally ranging from 60% to 80%, depending on the source. Plant proteins are often less complete in their amino acid profiles, meaning they may lack one or more essential amino acids. Factors like fiber, antinutrients (such as phytic acid and lectins), and other plant compounds can inhibit protein absorption. For muscle building you would have to eat three to four pounds of cooked lentils just to match the same protein from one pound of meat! Sorry, my vegan readers, but the carnivore diet is a better way of eating especially for building muscle. Make the switch today!

Eggs

"I know this may be a stretch, but can I start getting 14 dozen eggs? My kids are starting to enjoy eating them as well." I asked Shelby, my egg dealer, in a text.

"Let me see and I will let you know ASAP!" Shelby responded.

"What time can I pick them up tomorrow? Location?" I fired back.

"We can do 10 at the fire dept if that works! I think I will have 14 dozen for tomorrow as well!"

"Ok I'll be there thank you!"

Thus I increased my egg consumption to a dozen each day. When I first started the carnivore diet I was testing eating eggs. I switched my brain from eating carbs every morning like biscuits, pancakes, waffles, and cinnamon rolls, to meat like bacon, steak, and eggs. I found eggs to be extremely easy to cook, very palatable, and nutrient dense. It was the perfect food. I started making two dishes of six eggs each. One dish I would eat for breakfast, the second I would eat for lunch. Eventually I would eat twelve eggs every single day including my weekends and I never got tired of eating them.

Vince Gironda, known as the "Iron Guru," was a highly influential figure in the bodybuilding world during the mid-20th century. He was a strong advocate of eating large quantities of eggs, especially for muscle growth and strength development. Gironda believed that eggs, particularly whole eggs, were one of the best sources of protein and vital nutrients for bodybuilders.

He famously promoted a diet that included eating up to 36 eggs a day, claiming that this provided results comparable to the use of anabolic steroids due to the high levels of protein and fats, particularly cholesterol, which he believed supported testosterone production. Gironda's approach was unconventional but attracted many followers due to the impressive physique results his methods delivered.

Upon reading about Gironda I was sold. I had been eating eggs for a few months now and I was eating them more because it was so easy to budget, having gone through scorched earth in the aftermath of the EPO. When I found out about Gironda and the amount of eggs he was consuming it changed my worldview. I had a new respect for this little pot of nutritious gold and was only going to increase my intake from there. Thus twelve eggs became the standard and my diet became extremely healthy.

Eggs are such a staple in my diet I had to make a section devoted just to it. It's like the fountain of youth. Eggs are considered a nutritional powerhouse due to their rich content of essential nutrients, making them one of the best foods for health and wellness. Here's why eggs are so beneficial:

1. High-Quality Protein

Eggs provide all nine essential amino acids, making them a complete protein source. This protein is easily digestible and helps build and repair muscles, tissues, and cells.

2. Rich in Essential Vitamins and Minerals

Vitamins: Eggs contain several B vitamins (B2, B6, B12), which support energy production, brain health, and red blood cell formation. They're also high in vitamin D (essential for bone health), vitamin A (for vision and immune function), and vitamin E (an antioxidant).

Minerals: Eggs contain phosphorus, calcium, and selenium. Selenium is an antioxidant that helps protect the body from cell damage.

3. Choline Content

Choline is crucial for brain health, liver function, and cellular maintenance. It plays a role in neurotransmitter synthesis and is essential for pregnant women, as it supports fetal brain development.

4. Healthy Fats

Eggs contain both monounsaturated and polyunsaturated fats, which are beneficial for heart health. While they also have saturated fat, recent studies suggest that moderate intake doesn't significantly impact heart disease risk in healthy individuals.

5. Eye Health Benefits

Eggs are a good source of the antioxidants lutein and zeaxanthin, which help protect the eyes from age-related macular degeneration and cataracts.

6. Weight Management

Due to their high protein content, eggs can increase feelings of fullness and help control appetite, making them a great food choice for weight management.

7. Heart Health

Though eggs contain cholesterol, recent research has shown that dietary cholesterol does not significantly impact blood cholesterol for most people. The high-quality protein and healthy fats in eggs may contribute to balanced cholesterol levels and overall heart health.

8. Low in Calories

One large egg contains about 70-80 calories, making it nutrient-dense and suitable for many diet plans, whether you're trying to gain muscle or lose weight.

9. Versatile and Easy to Prepare

Eggs can be incorporated into almost any meal, making it easy to add protein, vitamins, and other nutrients to your diet. They can be prepared in various ways, such as boiled, scrambled, poached, or baked. For these reasons, eggs are not only a convenient and affordable source of nutrition but also a versatile addition to a balanced diet.

Eat Meat, Build Muscle

If there's two things I could tell my twenty year old self, concerning health and fitness, it would be to eat meat and build muscle. Now that I'm in my 40's I've come to realize 60 doesn't look too far away. I'm going to be an old man sooner than I think. Time will pass by faster than I realize and one day Jasher will be twenty. I wish I could go back in time and tell my younger self, "John. Eat meat, build muscle."

Nutrition and health has now become such a staple in my life that I can't imagine how I was ever okay on the Standard American Diet (SAD). McDonald's, Taco Bell, Pizza Hut... a lot of these foods are really poison on your longevity. They're not as good for you as eating whole foods and drinking water. If you can just stay away from those places you'll be far better off than your counterparts.

"Dad, I want up!" Jasher called to me as he stood next to the pull-up/dip station I had just bought. I wanted to get back into shape, but thought the kids could use it as they got older as well. I picked him up by the waist and brought his extended hands to the pull-up bar.

Jasher already knew how to do pull-ups. He must have either seen me do them in the past or he learned them in school. He quickly pulled himself up to his chin and went down again, and up again, and down again. They weren't proper form nor were they full ROM (Range of Motion). They were just really quick up and downs, but I didn't criticize him. I was just happy to see him wanting to do the exercise. Proper form could come later. It was good to see Jasher try.

With one last grunt Jasher pulled himself up as hard as he could and he was down. I carefully guided him to the floor, hands still around his waist. His brother and sister wanted to jump on too so I let them both. Maverick simply wanted to touch the ceiling so he pulled himself up and looked down at me laughing. Then Jubilee went up. She touched the ceiling multiple times, feeling tall, giggling all the way. It made me happy to get them physically engaged at such an early age.

In today's culture, when kids were hooked onto smartphones and tablets, my kids had a role model to look up to. A superman of sorts. Someone who could help them maintain a healthier way of eating and a constant encouragement to stay in shape. I was their beacon of hope in this world of darkness and I was going to steer their health on a great path of optimal living. I was going to be the embodiment of The Greatest Dad On Planet Earth.

SECTION III

VICTORY

CINDERELLA MAN

"If she wants to drag this out, I'm going to go scorched earth." I responded to my attorney's email.

He had asked me why the sudden change. Originally I was playing softball and trying to work with Katie. I had been playing it safe, constantly watching what I was saying. Never swearing at her. Never trying to involve a reaction. My brother had told me to try to take the high road because she could use it against me in court. I was to play nice and try to stay in the line. A good boy. Subservient to the demands of the court and keep to myself until this had all been over. Women have greater leverage my default in the family court and I needed to be on my best behavior.

Meanwhile Katie was acting a fool. She would curse at me in emails, go off script, drag my name through the dirt and accuse me of all sorts of false accusations. Even when I showed the evidence of her wrongdoing nothing was being done. She was never punished, never scolded, and never held accountable. I was being treated like a low life while she was being treated like an angel.

Not anymore. I was done playing nice game. I kindly told my brother to go screw himself, this was my life now. I was now going thermo nuclear.

I had had enough and I was no longer going to be the nice guy. The nice guy had died in the 40 days and 40 nights of trial and tribulation. I was a new man! My own man. I had changed and I wasn't going back. I had told her a number of times to not take my mercy as weakness. Well she pushed me to the brink and I was no longer going to play by her rules or anyone else's for that matter. This was my family, my children, my tribe. If I was going to pay anymore money to my attorney I was going to take everything I could from her and more.

Katie was broke. She used the money, from the sale of our house, to purchase a chest tattoo, a new car, and whatever else. The money was gone. Mine was too. As discussed before, I gave most of it away and a quarter was used to pay off the immediate debts of close family and payday loans. Another quarter was used to set up my new place to make it liveable for myself and my children. I had spent the money wisely while she went on a self glorifying spree. I knew she didn't have much money so I switched to offense and attacked.

My plan was simple. I was going to push for child support. On paper this doesn't seem like that big of a deal, but in reality it was game changer. I knew Katie wouldn't be able to make the child support payments. I didn't want her money, I wanted the kids. They would be safe with me. They would be loved with me. They would grow up to be great contributions to society if they lived under my household than with her. She was just too much of a toxic role model to have my children live under.

Kick The Enemy When They're Down

"You have to dominate. You have to kill the competition. You have to go after them, and it's not a nice business." - Donald Trump, <u>Think Big: Make It Happen in Business and Life</u>

"Six hundred eighty dollars." The clerk told Katie.

"There must be some mistake. We thought the daycare was provided for free. Can you look at the math again?" Katie responded. She was with her attorney.

The accountant looked over the math again and realized she had a decimal wrong in the equation. She re-did the math and sure enough she was gave them the wrong number.

"I apologize for that. It's actually eight hundred forty dollars." The accountant replied back unapologetically.

Katie was devastated by the final total. Once again she spoke too much. She didn't know when to shut up. Had she kept her mouth shut the first time she wouldn't have to pay an extra two hundred dollars. Once again she shot herself in the foot. Through this entire nightmare of a divorce she would continue to shoot herself in the foot many times. Today was no different.

We had been summoned to the child support hearing where the accountant would figure out how much Katie would have to pay each month. It was solely because I had filed for child support that we were there. Had I not gone out of my way to put in the extra work, Katie would not be required to make any payments to me. Even though I had supported the children all by myself over the last year, unless you actually go through the required state child support system and finish all the paperwork, women pretty much get a magic pass on paying anything. Family court will always favor the women.

Katie's attorney asked if she could have a minute with Katie. With the accountant's permission they went into the hall. Now during this entire time the accountant had no idea of any back story to why I was filing for child support. Through this entire exchange I had not taken one look at Katie. I still remembered the Johnny Depp trial with Amber Heard; how he said he would never look at Heard in the eyes ever again. I felt the same. I couldn't look at her. She brought me through a personal hell of cheating and getting me removed from my children under a blatant lie. I also would never look at her in the eyes ever again if humanly possible.

"I never wanted a divorce." I whispered to the accountant. "She cheated on me multiple times and abandoned the kids. I had to."

I don't know if I was trying to gain empathy or make her understand the why. You have to see it through the family court's eyes. Women initiate divorce over seventy percent of the time. That leaves men at less than thirty percent filing for divorce. While precise statistics on how many men who initiate divorce file for child support are limited, studies indicate that men are less likely than women to file for child support, even when they have custody. Data from the U.S. Census Bureau shows that only about 17% of custodial fathers receive child support payments, compared to 54% of custodial mothers.

Katie and her attorney came back into the room and sat down. I still sat there, staring straight into the paperwork; never looking up. Her attorney told the accountant they could do two hundred and asked for an extension. At this point I had all the leverage. It would be up to me if I wanted to show her mercy or go after her for the full amount. I had every right to push the eight hundred dollars. After all, I had single handedly taken on all the burden of child care, spending well over one thousand dollars every month for day care and after school programs. The eight hundred wouldn't cover their every day essentials, but it would help alleviate some of the weight.

I remembered how it felt to barely make it every day. The countless days I would be on the verge of not having enough money to pay for gas to see my kids. Simply getting enough money for food for me to survive and make sure the kids were fed as well. How I had to donate plasma just to make ends meet and how I had to sell the number one instrument, my harp, just so I could finally reach the end. How hard those days were. It felt like a nightmare looking back; unreal and a volatile time of trial and tribulation.

Proverbs 25:21-22 KJV — If thine enemy be hungry, give him bread to eat; and if he be thirsty, give him water to drink: For thou shalt heap coals of fire upon his head, and the LORD shall reward thee.

As evil as Katie had been to me, I was not the same. My moral integrity would not allow me to return evil with evil. I was better than her in that regard. I would take the high road yet again. I decided to stretch out an olive branch even at this last moment. I would give mercy once more. I thought if I showed mercy one last time there was a chance this would bend her enough to finally sign over full custody. My bet would soon pay off.

Cinderella Man

There's a great movie called <u>Cinderella Man</u>. Cinderella Man (2005) is a biographical sports drama based on the life of James J. Braddock, a once-promising boxer who falls into poverty during the Great Depression. After struggling to provide for his family, Braddock makes a miraculous comeback to the ring, fighting against all odds to win the heavyweight championship. His resilience and determination make him a symbol of hope for those enduring hardship. The film stars Russell Crowe as Braddock and Renee Zellweger as his supportive wife, Mae.

Looking at this chapter of my life I like to think of myself as the character from Cinderella Man. I had gone through hell and survived. By the time this book gets published I will have been on this earth for forty years. During these forty years never, in my life, have I gone through such challenging times as I had this. I fought so hard to claim victory of my kids and finally made it to the end. Through literal blood, sweat, and tears I was finally at the finish line, champion to a time of devastation and insurmountable odds. I won.

We were supposed to meet at a trial date. My attorney and I would stand in opposition to my wife and her attorney. I would present my case as to why I want full custody and she would present her defense as to why she should have joint custody. It would be a fight I would be willing to take on until forever if necessary. It was a hill I was willing to die on. Katie was not a good person and I did not want my children to be neglected ever again. They didn't deserve that. In this world they were my everything.

That trial never happened. With the pressure from the child support she finally caved. She would sign over full custody in exchange for never having to pay any child support ever again. It's what I wanted. That was my original plan. I never wanted her money, I wanted my kids. I knew she wouldn't be able to take care of them so I wanted to give her a clean slate. I would take on all the financial responsibilities necessary to take care of all three children as well as all our marriage debts. I would happily pay them all off, I just wanted the children.

She signed the divorce papers and sent them off. I would retain full custody and she could have bi-weekly visitation. I would take care of all their medical expenses, food, clothing, shelter, etc. Pretty much what I've always been doing up to this point. I had no help financially from the government. I never received food stamps. All their child care necessities came out of my own pocket. I had done it all. By the grace of God I was able to take care of them all on my own. My children, my tribe, my peace.

It took a little back and forth, but the divorce finally came to a close. On June 3, 2024, at 2:54 pm, my divorce was finalized and I was free. I had been at war with my now ex-wife for over a year. All I wanted were my kids. I didn't care how many men she slept with now, I didn't care how she spent her money, I just wanted my kids. And they were finally mine. All my hard work and perseverance paid off. They were mine, they were loved, and I had finally won.

Graduation

"I'm so proud of you, son! How does it feel?" I asked Jasher proudly.

"Good!" Jasher replied back with the biggest smile on his face. It was May 14, 2024 and Jasher was graduating kindergarten today! He was dressed up in an all blue graduate attire with a gold tassel hanging from his cap. Blue was the primary school color and every child was dressed for success. It was a monumental moment for my son. He had come such a long way from the time he was just a baby.

We had been through a lot, him and I, and I was his #1 cheerleader. It had been such a difficult road to travel on, but it was all worth it in the end. Strangely it struck me as odd that Jasher never did once ask about his mother. The entire year Jasher had visitations every other week or so and he never asked about seeing his mom. Even when I called her on the phone, Jasher did not want to talk to her. We were at graduation now and Jasher didn't ask where his mother was. It wasn't even a thing that crossed his mind.

It was just me and his mother-in-law, sitting in the crowd, cheering him on as he walked down center stage and stood in a line with his peers. Maverick and Jubilee were also sitting with me, Maverick enjoying sitting in my lap while Jubilee being frustrated not being able to get out of the row of seats we were a part of. Jubilee tried hard to get out and run around to no avail.

"Jasher Baldwin!" The principal read out his name on the intercom. He got up to take his diploma. I cheered out a loud and steady cheer. He was an example of what could be done in such a negative circumstance. He was my bastion of hope in this dark world. My strength, my determination, my son. He meant the world to me. And now he was graduating. It had been a long road and I could rejoice during this moment of achievement.

They finished calling the rest of the names from the different classes and grade levels. Jasher sat back on stage in his seat, looking out at the audience then down to his diploma and back to the audience again. When they were done all the kids got up and walked back up the aisle to an area in the back of the school where I could go out and meet him and congratulate him in person.

"My dad!" Jasher saw me. I went back stage and waved at him. Then we took pictures and I walked him back to the front area where he could see his grandma and siblings. We all were very proud of him and this day of accomplishment. Jasher felt it too. They had a backdrop where you could take a picture with your child for graduation. I told him to stick up his index finger in the air in the sign of a #1. I did as well. With a big smile on my face we were victors together.

Father's Day

"Everyone say cheese!" My neighbor called out to us.

I was on bended knee. My kids were all on me. Jubilee was on my front side, sitting on my left lap. Maverick held on to my right side, legs wrapped on my right lap. Jasher was on my back, one arm wrapped half way around my neck. I had a big smile on my face, one finger pointed in the air as a sign of #1. My neighbor took a picture for me on my phone.

It was to be submitted to my work photo collage. KAAP was asking for Father's to send in their photos to be shown on the screens at work. There were a bunch of TV's in the break room and a few of them had current events going on at KAAP. One of them was a father's day tribute for all the dads. Many of the pictures had pictures of their entire family, wives included. I was one of the few with only myself and my children. To me it was an accomplishment that symbolized the hardship I went through as a dad, as a father, as a hero to my children. I was the hero they deserved and I was standing in the gap as victor over fate itself.

This Father's Day was more meaningful. Jasher's seventh birthday had just passed on June 15. Today was June 16. I felt my whole fight was more for Jasher than anyone else. From before I met his mom, I had written that one song. Then, one year after the song had been written and uploaded to YouTube, Jasher was born. Seven years from that day I was holding Jasher and his two siblings in my arms declaring victory. You couldn't tell me it wasn't a God-given victory. God was surely in the writing and Jasher was evidence of His authorship.

My war was finally over. I had won all the battles and eventually the entire war. I stood firm on my ground and did not give an inch to the enemy. Along the way there were many people that helped me out along the way and I had one that I needed to thank immediately, my attorney.

Even though he didn't do much after the EPO court, he still played a pivotal role in my win. Without his representation I strongly believe I would have never won. As I've stayed multiple times throughout this book, family court favors the women. It's rare that a man will win full custody of his children. The woman has to royally mess up big time for this to happen. And royally she did.

I went on Google Maps and gave a review for their business along with the Father's Day picture my neighbor had taken:

"When I found out my wife was cheating on me I knew I had to get a good lawyer because, if you're a man, you're going to lose by default in today's family court. I hired Keith Wilcutt to represent me. The day I filed for divorce is the day my wife filed a false EPO against me saying I was a violent man. I got kicked out of my own house and home for 40 days and 40 nights and could only see my kids for 2 hours each day. Because Mr. Wilcutt represented me not only was the EPO dropped, but I ended up getting full custody of my three children (2, 3, & 5 at the time). If you're a man, hire Keith Wilcutt. If you're wife cheated on you, hire Keith Wilcutt. If you go into family court with no lawyer, you're a moron and deserve everything that will happen to you next. You will lose. Hire Keith Wilcutt if you want to win."

First Grade

"Here we are! Start of a new school year, Jasher! How do you feel?" I excitedly asked Jasher.

"Good!" Jasher didn't have much to say. Today was his first day of first grade. He had grown so much. It was hard to imagine he made it through kindergarten and was in a new class, a new year, a new start. Jasher made it and I was fully in support of him. I loved him dearly.

Jasher was seven years old now. Long gone were the days of changing diapers. Hard to image just one year ago he was still in diapers at age six. He had done such an amazing job in becoming his own person. This child I had envisioned before I ever met his mother was now in first grade. He was the reason for the song I wrote before he was ever born. "Still Learning" was a song that had resonated in my soul and in my heart for as long as he was alive. It still held true to this day. I was still learning, still growing, still maturing. But so was Jasher and I was so proud of him.

Here we were once again, sitting in the parked line of cars, waiting for his school to start. This time he was joined by his sister who was now attending Pre-K. Maverick was still at Little Sprouts Daycare. Unfortunately I made too much money and they didn't allow Maverick to start kindergarten yet due to being born in October. He would have to been five years old by August in order to be enrolled. Sadly he would have to stay at the daycare one more year. I know it really bothered him as he wanted to start as soon as he could. I had dropped him off before I drove the other two to school.

Jubilee was my angel and was accepted to Pre-K on the merit of her having a learning disability. She still could not put a full sentence together and was still talking in baby talk at the age of three. She still had the bluest eyes I've ever seen in my life and still looked like the vision I had of her when I was nineteen years old. Very beautiful young lady. I was determined to tell her I loved her every day.

No turning back.

The days became normalized and familiar as time went on. While the visitation agreement was to have the kids see their mother every two weeks, I knew that would never come to pass. Katie had a horrible reputation for keeping dates and rigidity. There was never any structure to her life. I distinctly remember being the primary force of nature that held the family together. It was my focused nature, that never waivered, that allowed Katie so much freedom to grow in our marriage. That structure was now gone and Katie was a shell of her former self.

I often tell people that divorce is like a death in the family. Once a divorce is final, the relationship is over, the person has moved on, there is no going back to that relationship, the person is dead. When I first met my wife I was fully convinced she was a Christian. My faith doesn't allow me to marry outside of Christianity or it would be considered unequally yolked. Looking back I now know that was wrong and either she was never a Christian to begin with or she fell off somewhere along the way and there was nothing I could do to change her course. Everyone will have to account for their own sins and Katie will have to give an account of hers when she meets her own maker.

Katie would eventually have her sentence dropped to house arrest. She had gone through many trials and extensions and the money, from the house sale, was gone. She had to pay her attorney fees for representing her so much. I honestly think her attorney was taking advantage of her. Instead of making the case come to a close as soon as possible, he would extend it to further dates. Mind you most attorneys charge up to $200 per hour. To represent you in court it would be a mandatory two hour expense. Or in my EPO case, it cost me $750 up front. I don't know how much she ended up paying her attorney, but I know it wasn't cheap.

Originally she was set for up to fifteen years in prison due to the three felony counts of wanton child endangerment, but eventually she got that reduced to less than two years and eventually down to house arrest for three months with the possibility of a three month extension if she wasn't on her best behavior. She had to pay $300 each month for an ankle bracelet and was restricted to her house and job at a local casino. She would get a two hour window every week to buy groceries. During this time she hardly saw the kids and had a reputation of seeing them once every two to three months.

During our entire marriage she never worked a job outside the home. Before I married her I told her I would love for her to be a stay-at-home mom and raise the kids while I went to work as the sole breadwinner. In total we were together for 6+ years and our marriage finally dissolved after 7. Due to her sin of adultery she lost everything. She lost the house, the car, and all of her children. She lost the easy life I had set for her. I was more than happy to have her never work a day in her life until the day she died had she never cheated on me. Well the Lord will not allow His children to be burdened by those who sin and God removed her blessing the minute she stepped out in infidelity.

As for me I was a changed man. I became more hardened at the heart when it comes to relationships. I also became more of a no man. I was no longer a "nice guy." This divorce would either kill me or I would have to adapt. And adapt I did. I became a one man army, capable of watching three small children and doing an amazing job at raising them up to be healthy and loved. To this day I get complimented frequently on how well my kids are. Often times my children are the most well-mannered, well-groomed, and well-respected among their peers. I am the biggest influence in their lives and I plan on making the best role model for them.

I developed a morning routine where I would wake up at 3 am every morning, work out for an hour, take a cold shower, then practice the piano for 45 minutes before starting my day and going back to sleep by 10 pm every night to repeat the day again. If I wanted to get in shape and practice music, I would sacrifice my own time to make it happen. I developed a new diet that worked for me. At the worst time of my divorce I was down to 123 lbs. Two years later I was back up to 148 and I plan on continuing until I hit 180 before I maintain at that weight for the rest of my life.

Kim would be a close asset to my family. I would visit her on almost a weekly basis so she could see her grandbabies. She played an integral role in my need when everything went to hell in a hand basket. We would celebrate holidays together and she would watch the kids grow. To this day she's amazed at how much hair Jubilee has grown. During my marriage Jubilee's hair didn't grow much and we both think it was due to the stress of neglect when their mother locked herself up in her room the whole day while I was at work. Now Jubilee was developing into an independent young lady. I was very proud of her growth.

Britany, the nanny, quit working for me after three months. She couldn't handle the stress from watching the kids full time as well as dealing with Katie and I don't blame her. She didn't have any days of vacation and was underpaid until I was able to gift her the $10,000 from the sale of the house. Shortly after I paid her and the EPO was dissolved she left to live her life. There's no greater person that deserves my gratitude than her. Without her help I have no idea how I would have made it. Thank you, Britany.

As for what the future holds it's still unclear. After I publish this book I'm going to publish the one song that started this all. If anything this has been a love letter to my oldest son, Jasher. Before he was ever born, God gave me a song. I wrote that song down. It was burning in my heart. Exactly one year later he was born. My first born son, Jasher Baldwin was born on June 15, 2017 and I was in love. He made my life worth living and he stuck with me through this entire trial and didn't complain once. His name means Upright and he's always a reminder of God's grace in my life.

Milestone

Jasher sat down in the passenger seat next to me. Jubilee was in my lap. We were parked in a line of cars, waiting for school to open at 7 am. Jubilee was moving back and forth while messing with the car stereo, pressing as many buttons as possible. Jasher was messing with the sun blocker, switched to messing with me, then tag teaming with Jubilee to see how many buttons he could press. They were both laughing and having a fun time, all at my demise.

I had often made it to their school with five minutes to spare. It was the perfect time frame. Not too early to get the kids restless, not too late to make them feel rushed. As in the year before, after drop off I would head to work. Only this time I had a confidence that everything would be alright. I still remember the first day I dropped Jasher off in kindergarten. Tears welled up in my eyes as I drove away from the school. They were tears of happiness, uncertainty, joy, and compassion wrapped all in one. I knew I was on the right path, I just didn't know what was ahead.

One year later we were finally here again. This time the feeling was different. I felt confident in who Jasher was and where he was going. I felt confident in who Jubilee was and where she was going. I felt confident in who Maverick was and where he was going. The air of uncertainty had passed and I only knew victory. The hardest time, in my entire life, was behind me. The only thing that laid ahead was a light that shined brighter than anything I had experienced before. Hope.

Throughout the writing of this book I shed many tears. There were many memories I had to recall that seemed like yesterday. I cried for the hurt I felt from betrayal, I cried for the pain I felt when my children were removed from me, I cried for the death of my relationship with my wife, I cried for the pain of tribulation from financial hardship and sacrifice, and I cried for the sheer amount of joy I felt the day I won my war, won my children, and won my freedom. This book has been the culmination of the hardest time in my entire life and it's finally come to its end. I hope it can be a great motivator in your own life as you become The Greatest Dad On Planet Earth.

"Seven o'clock! Time to go!" I said to Jasher and Jubilee. We drove up to the drop off point. I opened my door and let Jubilee out with a big hug and a kiss.

"Love you, Daddy!" Jubilee said with a minor lisp. She was doing better with her words, but still talked like a baby a lot of the times. She was making so much progress.

"Love you too, honey! You have a good day!" I called out as she walked to the front entrance. I closed my door and turned to Jasher to give him a big hug and kiss as well. One last hug and kiss before I headed out to work. One last time to tell him I loved him dearly. One last embrace with my first born son, my son of prophecy, Jasher Baldwin. Jasher hugged and kissed me back on the cheek. I loved him and he loved me.

"I love you, Dad!"

"I love you too, son! With all my heart!"

"Follow our journey at: facebook.com/thebaldwintribe"